# Much About Nothing

## by William Shakespeare

Warring!  Wooing!  Wordplay!  Weddings!  Much Ado About Nothing has it all.  Luckily, CGP is here to explain everything — characters, language, themes, historical background... the lot.

We've included bags of brilliant online extras too.  There's a free Online Edition, tailored activities for all the big GCSE exam boards, and quizzes to test you on the whole play!

### Unlock your free online extras!

Just go to **cgpbooks.co.uk/extras** and enter this code or scan the QR codes in the book.

2284 4103 4371 9354

By the way, this code only works for one person.  If somebody else has used this book before you, they might have already claimed the Online Edition.

# GCSE English
# The Text Guide

# Contents

# Contents

You'll see **QR codes** on the Practice Question pages, which you can scan with any device. They'll take you to a set of **Sudden Fail Quizzes** for *Much Ado About Nothing*.

There are separate quizzes for the **Plot**, **Characters**, and **Context, Themes & Techniques** — or you can try the **full quiz**, which combines all of these topics. Just scan the QR code to give it a go!

P.S. You can also find these quizzes at **cgpbooks.co.uk/muchadoquiz**

Sudden Fail Quiz

Published by CGP

*Editors:*
Andy Cashmore
Emma Crighton
Sophie Herring
Sam Summers
Matt Topping

*Contributor:*
Gemma Gilvin

With thanks to Siân Butler and Rebecca Ritson for the proofreading.
With thanks to Jan Greenway for the copyright research.

*Acknowledgements:*

*With thanks to Geraint Lewis for permission to use the front cover image and the image on page 4.*

*With thanks to Alamy for permission to use the images on pages 5, 6, 10, 23, 27, 29 & 30.*

*With thanks to Alastair Muir for permission to use the images on pages 11, 12, 19, 20, 22, 31, 34 & 53.*

*With thanks to ArenaPAL for permission to use the images on pages 8, 15, 16, 46 & 48.*

*With thanks to iStock.com for permission to use the image on page 1.*

*With thanks to Photostage for permission to use the images on pages 2, 3, 5, 7, 17, 18, 28, 33, 51 & 54.*

*With thanks to Rex Features for permission to use the images on pages 1, 3, 4, 26, 38, 39, 40, 41, 47, 49, 50 & 52.*

*With thanks to the Royal Shakespeare Company for permission to use the images on pages 3, 14, 21, 37, 42 & 43.*

*With thanks to Shakespeare's Globe for permission to use the images on pages 13 & 32:*

*Image on page 13: Eve Best as Beatrice and Charles Edwards as Benedick in Much Ado About Nothing, directed by Jeremy Herrin, at Shakespeare's Globe (2011). Photographer credit Manuel Harlan.*

*Image on page 32: Joseph Marcell as Leonato in Much Ado About Nothing, directed by Jeremy Herrin, at Shakespeare's Globe (2011). Photographer credit Manuel Harlan.*

*With thanks to TopFoto for permission to use the image on page 9.*

ISBN: 978 1 78294 851 3
Printed by Elanders Ltd, Newcastle upon Tyne.
Clipart from Corel®

# Introduction to 'Much Ado...' and Shakespeare

## 'Much Ado About Nothing' is a comedy about love

- *Much Ado About Nothing* is about **two couples** who fall in **love** in very **different** ways.

- Both couples end up getting **married**, but it's not an easy journey — they encounter **disagreements**, **deception** and **humiliation** along the way.

- The play continues to **entertain audiences** today — it combines **humour** and **romance** with comments on society and darker moments.

> *Much Ado About Nothing* is about love and marriage
>
> 1) Claudio and Hero have a **traditional** approach to **marriage** — Claudio decides to marry Hero based on her **beauty**, **reputation** and **status** in society.
>
> 2) Benedick and Beatrice are **unconventional** — they **ignore** society's **expectations** and are **opposed** to **marriage** at first. When they do fall in love, their relationship seems more real.

Don Pedro woos Hero

## Shakespeare is the most famous writer in the English language

- William Shakespeare wrote at least **thirty-seven plays** and a lot of **poems**.

- He wrote some of the most **famous** plays in the English language, including **comedies** (such as *Twelfth Night*), **tragedies** (such as *Romeo and Juliet* and *Hamlet*) and **histories** (such as *Richard III*).

- *Much Ado About Nothing* is one of Shakespeare's **most-performed** comedies.

- It was written between **1598** and **1599**. The Claudio and Hero story is **inspired** by **earlier** 16th century European **romances**, while the Benedick and Beatrice plot is probably **Shakespeare's** own **invention**.

| | |
|---|---|
| 1564 | Born in **Stratford-upon-Avon**, Warwickshire. |
| 1582 | Married **Anne Hathaway**. |
| 1583-85 | Had three children — Susanna, Hamnet and Judith. |
| 1585-92 | Began an **acting career** in **London**. |
| 1589-1613 | Wrote most of his plays. |
| 1600 | **'Much Ado About Nothing'** first published. |
| 1616 | Died, aged 52. |

# Background Information

## 'Much Ado About Nothing' is set in Messina — a city in Sicily

Most of the action takes place in **Leonato's house** and **garden**.  Here are the **key locations** in the play:

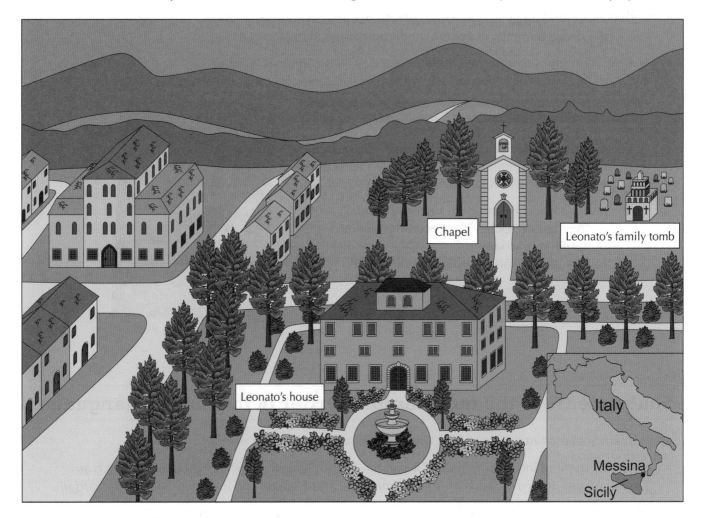

Chapel

Leonato's family tomb

Leonato's house

Italy

Messina

Sicily

## There's a joke in the play's title

© Donald Cooper / photostage

- In Shakespeare's time, the word '**nothing**' would have been **pronounced** like '**noting**' (which means 'observing').

- So *Much Ado About Nothing* has **two meanings**:
  'A lot of fuss over **nothing**' or
  'A lot of fuss caused by **noting**'.

- Shakespeare uses **jokes** and **puns** like this throughout the play.  **Puns** are jokes based on the **different meanings** of a **word** or words that **sound similar** — this play has lots of puns about **horns** and **sex** (see p.53).

- There is lots of **noting** in the play — many of the **deceptions** and **misunderstandings** are the result of characters **observing** each other.  These deceptions and misunderstandings have a **big impact** on the **plot**.

- The title also **hints** that the play will have a **happy ending**.  There will be **lots of drama** ('Much Ado'), but everything will be **fine** in the end because it will turn out that all the fuss was '**About Nothing**'.

# Who's Who in 'Much Ado About Nothing'

### Claudio...

... is a young count who falls in love with Hero. He is tricked into believing she has been unfaithful.

### Hero...

... is a quiet and obedient young noblewoman. She is falsely accused of being unfaithful to Claudio.

### Benedick...

... is a witty soldier who claims he will never marry. He is tricked into falling in love with Beatrice.

### Beatrice...

... is Hero's witty, strong-willed cousin. She is tricked into falling in love with Benedick.

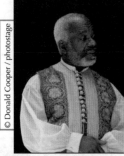

### Leonato...

... is the well-respected governor of Messina. He is Hero's father and Beatrice's uncle.

### Don Pedro...

... is the Prince of Aragon. He is responsible for bringing together both couples in the play.

### Don John...

... is Don Pedro's illegitimate brother. He is the villain of the play and causes trouble for the other characters.

### Dogberry...

... is the head of the Watch (the local police force). He is well-meaning but incompetent.

Introduction

# Plot Summary

## 'Much Ado About Nothing'... what happens when?

*Much Ado About Nothing* needs to be as familiar to you as your favourite socks. This little recap of the **main events** will help you on your way, but it's no substitute for reading the play. There's no escaping that I'm afraid...

## Acts One and Two — Don Pedro and his men arrive in Messina

© Clive Coote / Sam Goldwyn / Renaissance / BBC / Kobal / REX / Shutterstock

- **Don Pedro** has been **fighting** a **war** against **Don John**. He visits **Leonato** in Messina, along with **Claudio**, **Benedick** and **Don John**.

- **Claudio** falls in love with **Hero**. Benedick **mocks** Claudio for wanting to marry her, but Don Pedro agrees to **help** him **win** her over.

- **Beatrice** and **Benedick** enjoy **teasing** each other. They make **jokes**, throw around **insults** and both **scorn** the whole idea of **marriage**.

- Leonato throws a **masked ball**. Don Pedro **pretends** to be Claudio and flirts with Hero to **woo** her for him.

- Don John tries to **turn** Claudio **against** Don Pedro. He tells Claudio that **Don Pedro** wants **Hero** for himself, but Claudio soon finds out this **isn't true**. Leonato **agrees** that Claudio can marry Hero. Don Pedro decides to **set up** Beatrice and Benedick — he will **trick** them into **falling in love**.

- Meanwhile, Don John's companion **Borachio** suggests a scheme to make Claudio believe Hero has been **unfaithful** to him — this will **damage** Claudio's **reputation**, as well as Leonato's and Don Pedro's.

- Don Pedro, Claudio and Leonato make sure Benedick **overhears** a conversation about how Beatrice is in **love** with him. Benedick **believes** what he hears and realises he is **in love** with Beatrice.

## Act Three — Don John tricks Claudio

© Donald Cooper / REX / Shutterstock

- Hero and Ursula (her servant) continue Don Pedro's **plan**. They ensure that Beatrice **overhears** their conversation about Benedick's **love** for her. Beatrice is **excited** at what she **hears** and realises she **loves** Benedick too.

- Don John tells Claudio that if he goes to Hero's window that night, he will see her with **another man**. What Claudio sees is really **Borachio** with his lover, **Margaret**, but he **believes** she is Hero and is **furious**.

- Some of Dogberry's men **overhear** Borachio boasting about the **trick** played on Claudio. They **arrest** Borachio and his friend Conrade.

- Dogberry tries to tell Leonato that he has **arrested** Borachio and Conrade. He takes **too long** to explain and Leonato **leaves** for Hero and Claudio's **wedding** without finding out what has happened.

## Act Four — The wedding is called off

- Everyone comes together for Hero and Claudio's **wedding**. Claudio **accuses** Hero of being **unfaithful** — Hero tries to explain that she's **innocent**, but Claudio won't listen. She **faints** and Claudio **leaves** her.

- Leonato **believes** the accusations and is **furious** with Hero. Beatrice and the Friar both **defend** Hero — they believe she is **innocent**.

- The **Friar** proposes a plan — they should **pretend** that Hero is **dead**, which will allow **time** for the **truth** to come out. Leonato eventually **agrees**.

- Benedick and Beatrice **confess** that they **love** each other, but Beatrice is upset about Hero and wants **justice** for her. She asks Benedick to **kill** Claudio — Benedick agrees to challenge him to a **duel**.

- Dogberry attempts to **interrogate** Borachio and Conrade, but doesn't do a very good job. The **Sexton** (a church official) steps in and finally uncovers the **truth** about Don John's **plot** against Hero and Claudio. He also reveals that Don John has **fled**.

## Act Five — The truth is revealed and the couples are united

- Leonato is **upset** about the damage to Hero's **reputation**. Antonio encourages him to seek **revenge**. They **threaten** Claudio, but Claudio and Don Pedro **mock** the old men.

- Benedick **accuses** Claudio of **killing** Hero and **challenges** him to a **duel**. Claudio and Don Pedro **mock** Benedick and try to **joke** with him, but Benedick is **serious**.

- Dogberry brings his **prisoners** to Don Pedro and Claudio. Borachio **confesses** to the plot, which proves Hero's **innocence**. Claudio and Don Pedro **regret** what they did and feel **responsible** for Hero's death.

- Leonato keeps **pretending** that Hero is **dead**. He tells Claudio that he must marry Hero's '**cousin**' to **make up** for what he did. Claudio must also tell everyone she was **innocent** and **mourn** her at her tomb.

- At the wedding, the '**cousin**' reveals herself to be Hero, **alive** and well. She **forgives** Claudio.

- Benedick **proposes** to Beatrice. Hero and Claudio produce **love poems** that prove Benedick and Beatrice's love for each other. After some **arguing** and **teasing**, Beatrice **agrees** to marry him.

- Don John is **captured** and will be **punished** after the **weddings**. The play ends with **music** and **dancing**.

### Sounds like a bit more than nothing to me...

Once you're confident that you know what happens in *Much Ado About Nothing*, you're ready to start Section One. If you're still not sure about the plot or want a break from revision, have a look at the *Much Ado About Nothing* cartoon at the back of the book.

## How Plays Work

Lots of people will tell you that Shakespeare is the hardest thing you have to study for English — and they might be right... but it should be less hard and less weird when you've read everything in this section.

### 'Much Ado About Nothing' is meant to be watched — not read

1) *Much Ado About Nothing* is a **play**. A play tells a story by **showing** it to you.

2) When you **read** the play, it's often pretty hard to **follow** what's going on. Think about what the characters are **doing** and **imagine** how they would **speak** and **act** — it should all start to make a lot more sense.

3) If you can, try to see the play **on stage**. If not, watch a **film** version to get an idea of the **story**.

4) But remember to **read the play** as well — films often **cut scenes** and **change** the language, so it's **dangerous** to rely on them too much.

### Theatre was an important form of entertainment

The rebuilt Globe Theatre in London

1) There was no **TV**, **radio** or **internet** in Shakespeare's time, so going to the **theatre** was really popular.

2) The theatre wasn't just for **rich** people — Shakespeare's audiences included **servants** and **labourers**. Audiences could get quite **rowdy** during performances.

3) The **poorer** people in the audience stood in **front** of the stage — if it rained, they got wet. The **richer** people sat in the **covered galleries** above.

4) Shakespeare's theatre company, the **King's Men** (previously called the **Lord Chamberlain's Men**), performed in the **Globe Theatre** in London. This was **rebuilt** in 1997.

5) It was **illegal** for **women** to act, so the women's parts were played by young **boys** (even Beatrice...).

### 'Much Ado About Nothing' is a comedy

This play is one of Shakespeare's **most famous** comedies. Mostly, it's a **typical comedy**...

- It's about **love** and has a **happy ending** — both couples get **married**.
- There are lots of **disguises** and **mistaken identities**.
- It has **comic characters** who are **only** there to provide **humour**, such as Dogberry.

But there are also a few **less comic** things...

- It contains **tragic** elements, such as Hero being **shamed** at the wedding.
- Hero **fakes her own death** — this also happens in **tragedies** like *Romeo and Juliet*.
- **Don John's plots** cause **tension** and some **dark** moments in the play.

# How Plays Work

## Pay attention to the stage directions

When you're reading the play, look at the **stage directions** — they're little phrases in *italics* that tell the actors **what** to do, **when** to come in and when to **leave** the stage.

> These are the really **common** stage directions in **Shakespeare**:
>
> *Enter* = when someone **comes onto** the stage
>
> *Exit* = when one person **leaves** the stage
>
> *Exeunt* = when **more** than one person **leaves** the stage
>
> *Aside* = when a character **talks** to **themselves**, the **audience** or a **particular** character, but **not all** characters on stage can **hear**

## Understand what's happening on stage

© Donald Cooper / photostage

1) Try to **picture** what would be **happening** on stage — think about how the **actors** would **move** around and how the **stage** might **look**.

2) For example, at the masked ball, the **stage directions** tell you that there is **music** and **dancing** and the men are wearing **masks** — this makes the scene **exciting** and visually **dramatic**.

3) **Music**, **costumes** and **props** can be used to create different **effects**. They help create the **atmosphere** of a scene and can **influence** the audience.

4) Look for **clues** about **where** the actors would be on stage and **how** they might move around. For example, if a character is **overhearing** something, they would be **hidden** from the other characters but **visible** to the audience.

5) Benedick and Beatrice are both tricked in the **orchard** — they might be **hidden** behind **trees** or **bushes**, or any other **props** that are on stage. This is an opportunity to create **comedy** for the audience.

## Read lines aloud to get the jokes

1) Shakespeare's **lines** were meant to be **heard** rather than **read**. An **actor** delivers their lines in a **particular** way to show the character's **personality** or **emotions**.

2) Some lines make **more sense** when you read them **aloud** rather than in your head. This is because a lot of the **puns** and **humour** rely on the way the words **sound**.

3) Beatrice makes a **pun** about Claudio being **bitter** — she says he is as "**civil as an orange**", which sounds like 'Seville orange' (the Spanish city of Seville was known for its **bitter oranges**).

4) Reading **Dogberry's lines** aloud makes it easier to tell which **similar-sounding** word he means to say. He tells the Watch to "**be vigitant**" when he means 'vigilant' (observant).

---

### Remember that plays are written to be performed...

Shakespeare didn't expect people to sit at home reading his plays — he wrote them to be performed in a theatre. That's why it's all dialogue and not much description — use your imagination for the rest...

# How to Understand Shakespeare's Language

Shakespeare's plays can be more confusing than a fox and ferret convention, especially all the strange ye olde language. But there are certain ways of reading it so it makes more sense — here's how it's done...

## The play is written in poetry and prose

1) Some of the play is written in **poetry** (or **verse**) — but the poetry doesn't usually rhyme.

2) The poetry is the bits where all the lines are **roughly the same length**, and each line starts with a **capital letter**. It **looks like this:** ➡️

   > "My love is thine to teach. Teach it but how,
   > And thou shalt see how apt it is to learn
   > Any hard lesson that may do thee good."
   > Act 1, Scene 1

3) Most of the play is in **prose** — prose is normal sentences **without** any **set rhythm**.

4) **Poetry** is usually used in scenes about **romance**, like when Don Pedro promises to **woo** Hero for Claudio, or in **serious** scenes, such as when Hero is **shamed** at the wedding.

   *For more on poetry and prose, see Section 5.*

5) Characters with a **lower social status**, like Dogberry, **only** speak in **prose**.

## Don't stop reading at the end of each line of poetry

1) Even though each line starts with a capital letter, it **doesn't** mean it's a separate sentence.

2) Just **ignore** the capitals and follow the **punctuation**.

3) For example, there's **no full stop** here, so carry on to the next line:

   > "No, no, 'tis all men's office to speak patience
   > To those that wring under the load of sorrow,"
   > Act 5, Scene 1

© Pete Jones / ArenaPAL

## Look out for words in a funny order

1) Another reason Shakespeare can be **tricky** to understand is the **long complicated sentences**.

2) It's often hard because the **word order** is **unfamiliar**. It's easier to understand if you **change** the **order**. For example:

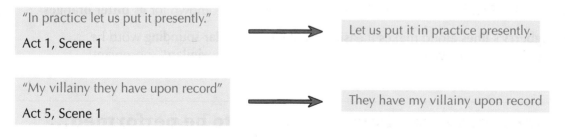

> "In practice let us put it presently."
> Act 1, Scene 1

➡️ Let us put it in practice presently.

> "My villainy they have upon record"
> Act 5, Scene 1

➡️ They have my villainy upon record

# How to Understand Shakespeare's Language

## You have to guess what the missing letters are

1) Shakespeare often **runs two words together** and misses letters out to make them fit into a line.

2) There's often an **apostrophe** instead of the **missing letter**. So "**I' faith**" means 'In faith'.

> I' faith, I thank him = In faith, I thank him

3) "**'tis**" is a **shortened** form of 'it is'. The **apostrophe** shows that there is a **missing letter** before the 't'.

> 'Tis certain so = It is certain so

4) If you come across random apostrophes when you're reading, try to **work out** what the missing letters are.

## Mind your thees, thous and thys

1) They had **different words** for 'you' in Shakespeare's time.

2) People used to say '**thou**' to be **familiar** or **friendly**, and '**you**' to be more **formal**. Look out for these words:

| Thou = You | Thy = Your |
|---|---|
| Thee = You | Thine = Your |

3) Benedick uses the informal '**thee**' when he tells Beatrice that he loves her.

> "I protest I love thee."
>
> Act 4, Scene 1

## And finally, some more old, confusing words

1) **Verbs** often look a bit **different** from the English used today...

| thou art = you are | thou wilt = you will |
|---|---|
| thou hast = you have | thou canst = you can |

2) If this seems difficult, here's a trick — **take the 't' off** the end of the **verb**:

> hast – t = has
>
> wilt – t = wil(l)

3) And here are a few more words to **watch out for**:

| hither | = | to here | wherefore | = | why |
|---|---|---|---|---|---|
| hence | = | away from here | ere | = | before |
| whither | = | where | nay | = | no |
| thither | = | to that place | by my troth | = | I swear |

## Spend some time getting to grips with the language...

So, Shakespeare missed letters from his words, and he put his words in a funny order. As annoying as that may be, you need to get used to it. The better you understand the play, the better you'll do in your exam.

# Section Two — Discussion of Acts

## Analysis of Act One — Claudio Falls in Love

This section analyses each scene of *Much Ado About Nothing* and tells you what's what. It covers all the main plot points — but make sure you actually read the play as well. Go on, you know it's important...

### Scene 1 — The soldiers arrive in Messina...

1) Leonato receives a message from Don Pedro — he's recently **won** a **war** and is coming to Messina.

2) Leonato is **pleased** to hear that Claudio **fought well** and earned a good **reputation** for himself. This introduces the importance of **honour** as a theme in the play.

3) Beatrice asks if there's any **news** about Benedick and **enjoys** confusing the messenger with her **wit**. Hero is also on stage, but remains mostly **silent**.

> **Characters — Hero and Beatrice**
>
> Hero's **silence** highlights the **contrast** between her and Beatrice. She is presented as **meek** and **submissive**, while Beatrice is **outspoken** and **confident**.

4) Beatrice's comments about Benedick are **critical** yet **amusing**, which introduces the "<u>merry war</u>" between them. This **oxymoron** sets up their **ongoing conflict** — they enjoy **arguing** with each other and are **equally matched** in **wit**.

> An oxymoron is a phrase that appears to contradict itself.

### ... Benedick and Beatrice bicker, and Claudio falls for Hero

© Geraint Lewis / Alamy Stock Photo

1) Don Pedro **arrives** with Claudio, Benedick and Don John. They are greeted **warmly** by Leonato — this sets up a **light-hearted mood** for the play in **contrast** to the **war** the men have just been fighting.

2) Beatrice **teases** Benedick and he replies just as **sharply**. She tells him no one is **listening** to him and he calls her "<u>Lady Disdain</u>". They acknowledge that they are **similar** — he has a "<u>hard heart</u>", she has "<u>cold blood</u>" and neither is interested in **romance**.

> **Theme — Love and Marriage**
>
> Benedick and Beatrice are both **cynical** about love. This **contrasts** with Claudio, who's depicted as a traditional **courtly lover** — he falls madly in **love** with Hero.

3) Claudio really wants to **marry** Hero — he describes her as "<u>the sweetest lady</u>". In contrast, Benedick believes Beatrice is **prettier** than Hero and makes **jokes** about how "<u>short</u>" Hero is.

4) Benedick speaks **mockingly** about **love** and **marriage** — he is **determined** to remain a "<u>bachelor</u>". Don Pedro suggests Benedick might **change** his mind — this **hints** at him later falling in **love** with Beatrice.

> **Theme — Gender**
>
> Claudio sees Hero as a "<u>modest young lady</u>". Elizabethan society expected women to be 'pure' — this affects the **treatment** of Hero and the **actions** of the other characters throughout the play.

> **Shakespeare's Techniques — Puns and Wordplay**
>
> Benedick is sure he won't get **married** — he tells his friends to "<u>pluck off the bull's horns and set them in my forehead</u>" if he ever does. There are lots of **puns** about **horns** in this play — in Shakespeare's time, people joked that a **cuckold** (a man with an **unfaithful wife**) would grow **horns** on his head (see p.53).

---

### "Can the world buy such a jewel?"

Claudio falls head over heels for Hero in Act 1, Scene 1. He's absolutely convinced that she is everything he's looking for in a wife. They haven't said a word to each other yet, but apparently that's not important...

# Analysis of Act One — The Plan to Woo Hero

Everyone is plotting something. You might as well get used to this — it happens once or twice in the play...

## Don Pedro has a plan

1) Claudio asks Don Pedro to **help** him woo Hero — this shows he **respects** Don Pedro and **values** his advice.

2) Claudio gives a **passionate** speech about his "**soft and delicate desires**" for Hero. He is presented as a conventional **romantic hero** — a young man madly in love.

3) Claudio seems **nervous** about love and **unsure** what to do — this **contrasts** with the image of him as a **brave** and **honourable** soldier at the beginning of Act 1.

4) Don Pedro is a **loyal** friend and devises a **plan** to help Claudio. At the **masked ball** that night, he will **disguise** himself as Claudio, **woo** Hero for him and get Leonato's **permission** to marry her.

> **Shakespeare's Techniques — Poetry and Prose**
>
> Claudio and Don Pedro speak in **blank verse** here — previously the scene was in **prose**. This shows the **seriousness** of Claudio's **love** and connects him with the **exaggerated**, **poetic** language of a traditional **courtly lover**.

## Scene 2 — Antonio thinks Don Pedro loves Hero

1) **Antonio** tells Leonato (his **brother**) that **Don Pedro** is in **love** with Hero. One of his men has **overheard** Don Pedro's plan to help Claudio and **misunderstood** it.

2) Leonato is **surprised** by the news, but is **honoured** because Don Pedro is a man of **status**.

3) Leonato says he will inform Hero, so "**she may be the better prepared for an answer**" — but she **doesn't** get a say in the matter, as it's her **duty** to do what her **father** tells her.

> **Theme — Deception and Misunderstanding**
>
> Misunderstandings, **tricks** and **overheard conversations** occur throughout the play — this is the **first** of many.

## Scene 3 — Don John starts plotting

1) Don John is **introduced** to the audience. He **complains** about how **miserable** he is and his **lack of freedom**.

2) He knows the other men **don't like** him — he uses a **metaphor** to describe himself as a "**canker in a hedge**". A "**canker**" is a **wild rose**, but it's also a type of **disease**.

3) He **hates** his **brother** (Don Pedro) and would rather be an **outsider** than a "**rose in his grace**".

© Photograph by Alastair Muir

> **Theme — Loyalty**
>
> Don Pedro has forgiven his brother and welcomed him back into his circle, but Don John remains **resentful** towards him.

4) He **admits** that he is a "**plain-dealing villain**". From the beginning, it's clear that he wants to **cause trouble** for the other characters.

5) Borachio tells Don John about Claudio and Hero's potential **marriage**. When Borachio explains Don Pedro's **plan** to **woo** Hero on Claudio's behalf, Don John decides to **ruin** their relationship.

---

**EXAM TIP**

## Comment on Shakespeare's use of prose and verse...

Look out for switches between verse and prose — mostly the characters speak in prose, but sometimes they use verse. Have a think about what the effects of this are and what it tells you about the characters.

# Analysis of Act Two — Marriage Talk and Masks

Hero and Beatrice get a lecture on marriage, and the men all pretend to be someone they're not.

## Scene 1 — Hero will marry but Beatrice won't

1) Leonato and Antonio discuss **marriage** with Hero and Beatrice. The men have clear **expectations** — they believe it is a **woman's duty** to get **married**.

2) Antonio expects Hero to **obey** Leonato — "**I trust you will be ruled by your father.**" Leonato makes it clear that if Don Pedro **proposes**, Hero **must accept** him.

**Theme — Love and Marriage**

Hero and her future husband will **inherit everything** from Leonato, so he wants to make sure she marries someone **suitable**. Beatrice displays a more **modern** approach to marriage — she says Hero should have a **choice** in the matter and be **happy** with the person she marries.

**Theme — Gender**

Beatrice is **criticised** for being **unladylike**, while Hero shows **traditional feminine** qualities — she is **obedient** and **dutiful** to her father. Like in Act 1, Scene 1, Hero **says very little** while Beatrice speaks **wittily** and gets **plenty of lines**.

3) The men **try** to treat Beatrice in the same way, but she doesn't **conform** to the **behaviour** that they **expect** from **women**. Leonato tells her she will **never** get a **husband** if she keeps behaving as she does and Antonio says she is "**too curst**" ('bad-tempered').

4) Beatrice **ignores** society's expectations by **arguing** back, using **sexual innuendo** and more **jokes**.

5) To prove her **lack of interest** in a **husband**, she says a man **with a beard** would be too **itchy**, but a man **without a beard** is "**less than a man**". Her **impossible demands** are **amusing** to the audience.

## The men wear disguises to the ball

1) Leonato throws a **ball** for his guests — the men all wear **masks**. This is the perfect opportunity for **trickery** and there is a **light-hearted** mood to the scene.

2) The characters pair off into **couples** and the **men** each **pretend** to be one of the other characters. The **women** seem to **see through** their disguises — they are presented as being **less easily deceived** than the men.

3) As promised, Don Pedro **pretends** to be Claudio and takes Hero to one side so they can "**speak love**".

4) Hero has **more lines** here than in previous scenes and her speech is **witty**. The **masked ball** gives her **freedom** — **expectations** are **less strict** because people are in **disguise**.

5) Minor characters use the **masked ball** as an opportunity for **fun** and this creates **comedy** for the audience.

© Photograph by Alastair Muir

**Theme — Deception and Misunderstanding**

Tricks and misunderstandings **drive the plot** of the play. The theme is particularly **prominent** in this scene — the **masks** are a **visual** representation of how the characters like to play **different roles** and **deceive** each other.

6) For example, Ursula **teases** Antonio because he repeatedly **denies** being Antonio even though she knows he is. This shows that some characters are more **skilled** in **deception** and that some are **easier** to **trick**.

**"Not till God make men of some other metal than earth."**

Beatrice is very independent — she doesn't have much time for men and is determined that she'll never get married. Call me an old romantic, but I've got a feeling that she might change her mind about that...

# Analysis of Act Two — Two New Plans

Don John's up to no good. His first shady scheme doesn't work out, but Borachio has an even sneakier idea.

## Benedick gets insulted...

1) Beatrice gleefully **insults** Benedick — he is **pretending** to be someone else, so it's difficult for him to defend himself. Beatrice seems to **know** it's him and insults him **intentionally**.

2) She seems **ruthless** — she calls Benedick "<u>the Prince's jester, a very dull fool</u>" and says that everyone **laughs** at him behind his back.

3) Later in the scene she says that Benedick "<u>won</u>" her **heart** in the past by using "<u>false dice</u>" — this suggests she has been **hurt** by him before, which could explain why she is so **unkind** to him here.

4) Their "<u>merry war</u>" has become **harsher**. Benedick seems genuinely **hurt** by what she says — he uses imagery of **war** to show the **pain** she has caused, saying "<u>every word stabs</u>". This shows he can be **vulnerable**.

© Manuel Harlan

## ... and Claudio can marry Hero

1) Don John puts his **plan** into action. He shows **cunning** and takes advantage of the **masks** — he **pretends** to believe that Claudio is Benedick. He tells 'Benedick' that Don Pedro **loves** Hero and is **wooing** her.

2) Claudio **believes** the lie and reacts **immaturely** — Benedick compares him to a "<u>poor hurt fowl</u>" **hiding** in the bushes, which suggests he is **sulking**.

3) Don Pedro is quickly proved to be a **loyal** friend — Leonato agrees that Claudio can **marry** Hero. Claudio looks **foolish** to the audience as he has shown how **changeable** and **jealous** he can be.

4) Don Pedro thinks Beatrice and Benedick would be **well-suited** and decides to **set them up**. This creates **anticipation** for the audience — they **wonder** whether the plan will **succeed**.

### Shakespeare's Techniques — Poetry and Prose

Claudio has a **monologue** in **blank verse** when he thinks Don Pedro has wooed Hero for himself, and Benedick has one in **prose** after Beatrice insults him. This shows how they **react differently** — Claudio is **emotional** and **dramatic**, while Benedick is more **rational** and **considered**.

### TARGET GRADE 8-9

Keep a lookout for the play's many classical references. In this scene, Shakespeare uses one to provide humour — Don Pedro compares the task of matchmaking Beatrice and Benedick to "one of Hercules' labours". (Hercules was a mythological hero who completed twelve very difficult tasks called 'labours'.)

## Scene 2 — Borachio suggests a new plan

**KEY SCENE**

1) After the **fun** of the masked ball and the "<u>joy</u>" of the engagement, a sense of **threat** emerges as Don John starts **plotting** again.

2) Borachio suggests another **scheme** — Don John will claim that Hero has been **unfaithful** to Claudio so that he will **call off** the wedding. Claudio couldn't marry someone "<u>contaminated</u>" — this would **damage** his **reputation**.

### Context

In Shakespeare's time, people believed a woman should be a **virgin** until she got **married**. The same expectations didn't apply to **men**. A **modern** audience would consider this to be very **sexist**.

## Learn about Shakespeare's use of imagery...

Shakespeare sprinkles similes, metaphors and bits of personification across his writing like pepperoni on a pizza. Find some examples of imagery and think about the effects they have. See p.52 for more on this.

# Analysis of Act Two — Benedick is Deceived

Don Pedro's trick works wonders — Benedick has a pretty sudden change of heart about Beatrice...

## Scene 3 — Don Pedro and his friends trick Benedick...

*(KEY SCENE)*

1) Benedick has a **soliloquy** about **love**. He says Claudio is a **fool** to fall in love with Hero when he has **laughed** at other men for falling in love.

*See p.51 for more about soliloquies.*

2) He feels Claudio has **changed** since falling in love. He **contrasts** the life of a **soldier** with a **courtly lover**:

- Claudio used to be interested in "**good armour**", but now he prefers "**the fashion of a new doublet**".
- He used to "**speak plain**", but now his words are **poetic** and **dramatic** like a "**fantastical banquet**".

3) Benedick doubts he'll **ever** be like "**Monsieur Love**" (Claudio), but he does **list** the **qualities** of his **ideal woman** — these include being "**fair**", "**wise**" and "**virtuous**".

4) Leonato, Claudio and Don Pedro enter the **orchard** and Benedick **hides**. Balthasar sings a **song** that says "**Men were deceivers ever**" — the **male** characters have already **proved** this. Even so, it's **Hero** (who is telling the **truth**) that they later accuse of being a **liar**.

### Shakespeare's Techniques — Dramatic Irony

The **audience knows** that this is all a **trick** and Beatrice hasn't really said any of these things. This helps make the scene **humorous**.

*Dramatic irony is when the audience knows something that a character doesn't.*

5) The men put their **plan** into action — they know that Benedick is **hiding** and can **hear** every word they say, so they talk about how Beatrice is in **love** with him.

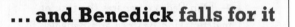

6) Benedick thinks he is doing the deceiving (by **eavesdropping**), but in fact the other three are **deceiving** him.

## ... and Benedick falls for it

1) Benedick wonders if this is a **joke**, but by the end he is **sure** that it **can't** be a **trick**. He **trusts** their 'evidence' (Hero 'told' them it was true) and doesn't think that an **honourable** man like Leonato would **lie**.

2) Benedick **changes his mind** about **marriage** and about **Beatrice** once he thinks she is in love with him. In another **soliloquy** about love, he says Beatrice is "**fair**", "**virtuous**" and "**wise, but for loving me**" — just as he described his **ideal woman** earlier in the scene.

### Shakespeare's Techniques — Setting

The **orchard** is a great **setting** for **deception** and 'noting' — there are lots of places to **hide**. Some directors have Benedick hiding in a **tree** so he can **overhear** the conversation, which creates **humour** for the audience.

3) Beatrice calls Benedick for dinner — Don Pedro has **sent** her so he can **test** Benedick's **feelings** for her.

4) She **insults** Benedick, but he replies much more **politely** than usual. He is sure he can see "**some marks of love in her**" — even though she is treating him the **same** as she always does. The **trick** has **worked**.

### Write about Shakespeare's use of dramatic irony...

*(EXAM TIP)*

Dramatic irony is put to good use in this play. Think about how it works with the theme of deception and misunderstanding to create humour. This is a comedy, after all, so hopefully you've had a few laughs...

# Analysis of Act Three — Beatrice is Deceived

It's Beatrice's turn to be tricked by her friends, so it's back to the orchard for another overheard conversation.

## Scene 1 — Hero and her friends trick Beatrice...

KEY SCENE

1) Hero **organises** the **plan** to **trick** Beatrice. Margaret will tell Beatrice that Hero and Ursula are in the orchard **talking** about her — Hero knows that Beatrice does actually **care** what people **think about her** and won't be able to resist coming to **listen**.

2) Beatrice **hides** in the **orchard** (just like Benedick did) so that she can **overhear** their conversation.

3) The women use **hunting imagery** when they talk about their plan for Beatrice. Ursula **compares** her to a "<u>fish</u>" who will "<u>greedily devour the treacherous bait</u>" and afterwards says they have "<u>caught</u>" her.

© Nigel Norrington / ArenaPAL

### Shakespeare's Techniques — Imagery

When Benedick is tricked, Claudio also uses **hunting imagery**, such as "<u>stalk on</u>". The men see themselves as **playing** the role of **Cupid**, who **shoots** his **arrows** to make people fall in love.

4) Hero and Ursula speak in **verse** when they talk about how Benedick is in **love** with Beatrice. When the men tricked Benedick, they spoke in **prose**. This suggests that the women's trick is **more sincere** and this scene is intended to be **less comedic** than the previous one.

5) Hero says that Beatrice always **rejects men** and finds **fault** in them — even "<u>So rare a gentleman</u>" as Benedick. She describes Beatrice as **proud**, **mocking** and **critical**.

6) She **knows** that Beatrice can **hear** her and takes the opportunity to **criticise** her — just as Don Pedro can't resist **insulting** Benedick in Act 2, Scene 3.

### Character — Hero

In previous scenes, Hero hasn't **spoken** much. Here Shakespeare shows a **different side** to her character — she is in **charge** of the plan, she **enjoys** the trick and even **criticises** Beatrice. She is more **confident** with **no men** around.

## ... and Beatrice falls for it

1) Beatrice **believes** what she has **overheard**. Like Benedick, she expresses her thoughts in a **soliloquy** at the end of the scene — she asks **questions**, her **tone** is **serious** and she speaks in **verse**.

### Shakespeare's Techniques — Structure

This scene **mirrors** Act 2, Scene 3 — the **setting**, the **imagery**, the **insults** and the **outcome** are all **similar**. These parallels highlight the similarities between Benedick and Beatrice, and their **changing** approaches to **love**.

2) This is very **different** from how she normally **speaks** — Shakespeare does this to reflect her intention to **change** for Benedick.

3) Once she thinks Benedick is in **love** with her, she realises she feels the same way about him. She says he could tame her "<u>wild heart</u>" and even suggests she would **marry** him — even though she has been **against marriage** before now.

KEY QUOTE

## "Some Cupid kills with arrows, some with traps."

People fall in love in different ways. Sometimes they realise it themselves, sometimes they just need to hide in an orchard and be tricked into it by their friends. Or that's what works for this lot, anyway...

# Analysis of Act Three — Claudio is Deceived

Borachio ignores the first rule of being a cunning villain — don't shout about your top-secret plans in public.

## Scene 2 — Benedick is in love...

1) Benedick is **quieter** and more **serious** than usual — he claims the **change** in mood is because he has "<u>toothache</u>". Don Pedro and Claudio **tease** him about being **in love**.

2) He has also **shaved** and is wearing **perfume** — these are things associated with **courtly lovers** (see p.39).

**TARGET GRADE** 8-9

The characters' personalities are often fluid and changeable. Benedick acts differently after he falls in love, just as Hero changes when she is with Ursula. You could argue that this makes it hard to tell when the characters are being authentic and when they're performing, which makes the play's deceptions even more unpredictable.

## ... and Don John tricks Claudio

**KEY SCENE**

© Pete Jones / ArenaPAL

1) Don John tells Claudio that Hero has been **unfaithful** and he will show him **proof** of her "<u>wickedness</u>".

2) Claudio says that if this is true, he **won't marry** Hero and will "<u>shame</u>" her during the **ceremony**. Don Pedro will join him — it is an **insult** to his **honour** as well.

3) Claudio quickly **believes** Don John, even though they don't like each other — this shows how **suspicious** he can be. He is concerned about **protecting** his **reputation** and this is **more important** to him than Hero.

4) Don John's plot provides a **threat** to the **comedy**. The audience expects a **happy ending**, but they also expect **obstacles** along the way — these create **tension** and make the happy ending more **satisfying**.

## Scene 3 — Borachio and Conrade are arrested

1) After the **darker tone** of the previous scene, Shakespeare introduces **Dogberry** and his assistant **Verges** to provide **humour** and **lighten** the **mood**.

*See p.33 for more on malapropisms and Dogberry's language.*

2) Dogberry is **incompetent** — he tells the Watch to **stay away** from criminals and **ignore** any crimes. His speech is **confused** and full of **malapropisms**, for example he says "<u>senseless</u>" when he means 'sensible'.

3) The Watch **overhear** Borachio **boasting** about the **trick** he played on Claudio, saying that Don John paid him a "<u>thousand ducats</u>" for it.

4) The trick itself takes place **offstage** — Borachio fills the audience in on what happened. Claudio **believed** that Margaret was Hero and was "<u>enraged</u>".

**Context**

There was no **police force** in Elizabethan England, so the Watch were supposed to **prevent crimes**. Most people thought they were **useless**, so Shakespeare's audience would have found it **amusing** to see the Watch **save the day**.

5) The Watch **arrest** Borachio and Conrade. They uncover the **truth** about Don John's plot **accidentally** because they **misunderstand** what has happened — this is **ironic** in a play with so much **deception**.

6) This creates **hope** for the audience, but also **tension** — they don't know if the **truth** will come out **in time**.

**KEY QUOTE**

## "every one can master a grief but he that has it."

While lovesick Benedick mopes around, his friends give him mocking advice to help his 'toothache'. He tells them that giving advice to others is easy, but taking it yourself is a different matter. So true...

# Analysis of Act Three — Wedding Preparations

Hero gets ready for a wedding that won't happen. Dogberry could save the day, but can't get his words out.

## Scene 4 — Hero gets ready for the wedding

1) Hero is preparing for her **wedding** and discusses her **outfit** with Margaret.

2) There is an **uneasy** atmosphere in this scene and a sense of **foreboding**:

> Foreboding is a feeling that something bad is going to happen.

- Shakespeare's use of **dramatic irony** makes the scene quite sad — the audience knows that Claudio **isn't** going to **marry** Hero and the women are preparing for something that isn't going to happen.
- Hero says "<u>my heart is exceeding heavy</u>", which **hints** at the **pain** and **drama** to come.
- Beatrice isn't her **usual self**. She says she is feeling **unwell** and is **impatient** with Margaret.
- Margaret **teases** Beatrice about being in **love** and makes **sexual jokes**, but this fails to lighten the mood — Hero **doesn't approve** of the jokes and Beatrice **refuses** to **admit** that she's in love.

3) Beatrice's behaviour **mirrors** Benedick's in Act 3, Scene 2. They both use **physical illness** as an excuse for behaving **differently** and they're both **teased** by their friends for being in love, which hints they are **meant** to be **together**.

4) Ursula reports that "<u>all the gallants of the town</u>" have **arrived** to take Hero to **church**. This highlights **how many** people will be at the wedding and suggests that Hero will face **public humiliation** when Claudio **rejects** her.

**Character — Margaret**

Margaret helps Hero get ready for a wedding that she has **helped** to **ruin**. She's **unaware** of her part in Don John's **plan**.

## Scene 5 — Dogberry tries to tell Leonato the truth

1) Dogberry and Verges take a **long time** to tell Leonato about their **prisoners** (Borachio and Conrade). Leonato is **polite** at first, but he is in a **hurry** to get to the **wedding** and quickly becomes **impatient**.

2) Dogberry and Verges **bicker** with each other, **babble** about what they want and **misunderstand** everything.

3) They brought **humour** earlier in Act 3, Scene 3, but now Leonato finds them "<u>tedious</u>" and their incompetence is **frustrating**.

4) This is a **missed opportunity** for the **truth** to come out. If Dogberry had properly explained who the prisoners were and what the Watch overheard them saying, Leonato could have **stopped** Claudio **accusing** Hero at the wedding.

© Donald Cooper / photostage

Hero hasn't been accused of anything yet, but the audience already knows that someone has the **evidence** to prove she **is innocent**. This reassures them that the misunderstanding will be **resolved**.

However, there is still **tension** for the audience — they **don't know** what's going to happen **before** the truth comes out. The audience **suspects** that things are going to get **worse** before they get **better**.

**KEY QUOTE**

## "methinks you look with your eyes as other women do."

Beatrice sees herself as being different from other women who are happy to settle down with a husband. But Margaret sees right through her — it's obvious that Beatrice is in love, even if she won't admit it.

# Analysis of Act Four — The Wedding

It's Claudio and Hero's wedding day, but something tells me they won't get their happy ending just yet...

## Scene 1 — Claudio accuses Hero...

**KEY SCENE**

1) Everyone has assembled for the **wedding** ceremony. When the Friar asks Claudio if he has come to marry Hero, Claudio says "**No**".

2) Hero **blushes**. This is a sign of her **innocence**, but Claudio **misunderstands** and says "<u>Her blush is guiltiness, not modesty</u>".

3) Claudio accuses Leonato of trying to "<u>Give</u>" him a "<u>rotten orange</u>" — this **metaphor** shows that he thinks Hero is **beautiful** on the outside but **rotten** on the inside.

> **Theme — Gender**
>
> Claudio's accusation makes it sound as if Hero is a **possession** and the marriage is a **transaction** between him and Leonato. He gets **angry** with Leonato **before** Hero — he holds the father **responsible** for the daughter.

4) Claudio uses **antithesis** and calls Hero "<u>most foul, most fair!</u>" He is shocked that someone who **seemed** so **innocent** could have **deceived** him like this.

*See p.54 for more on antithesis.*

5) He speaks **forcefully** to Hero and Leonato — he's **certain** that he is **right**. This **aggressive** approach **contrasts** with some of his previous behaviour, such as when he was too **nervous** to woo Hero himself.

> **Shakespeare's Techniques — Poetry and Prose**
>
> The scene begins in **prose**, but Claudio speaks in **verse** as he accuses Hero. This adds **drama** and reflects the **seriousness** of the scene. It also suggests that Claudio believes he is **noble** and doing the **right thing** — he sees himself as the **romantic hero** who has been **betrayed**.

6) Claudio is **convinced** he has been deceived. This is **ironic** — he has been **deceived**, but he can't see that he is **blaming** the **wrong** person (Hero) and **trusting** the wrong person (Don John).

7) Hero is **shocked** and tries to **defend** herself. She asks Claudio several **questions**, which shows how **confused** she is by the accusations.

## ... and Hero faints

1) Hero "<u>swoons</u>". This is a **visually dramatic** moment and the audience sees the **impact** of Claudio's accusations on her. Beatrice and Benedick **help** her, but Claudio **leaves** with Don Pedro and Don John.

2) Beatrice tries to **defend** Hero, but Leonato is **furious** with her. He knows that Claudio and Don Pedro are **well-respected** men and thinks they **wouldn't lie**. He uses images of **metal** in his speech — "<u>barred up with ribs of iron</u>" — to show how **strong** their claims are.

© Donald Cooper / photostage

> **Character — Leonato**
>
> Up to this point, Leonato has been **dignified** and **mature**. In this scene, there is a drastic **change** in his behaviour — he is **rash** and **passionate**.

3) Leonato even says Hero would be better off **dead** than living with this **shame**, which has 'stained' her forever (see p.26). His speech is **self-pitying** and full of **questions** that show his **despair**. It's as though she really has **died** and he is **grieving**.

## Mention the tragic mood of this scene...

**EXAM TIP**

This scene could belong in a tragedy — there's nothing to laugh at here. The language is very harsh as the men gang up on Hero (even her own father). She's confused and devastated by their accusations.

# Analysis of Act Four — Hero Plays Dead

Friar Francis has an, um, interesting solution to Hero's problems — definitely don't try this one at home...

## The Friar has a plan

© Photograph by Alastair Muir

1) Friar Francis **defends** Hero — he has been "**noting**" her and believes that she is "**guiltless**". This is a **rare** occasion in the play when someone **notes** something and sees the **truth** rather than being **deceived**.

2) Hero **protests** that she is **innocent** — she speaks **passionately** and **at length** for the first time in the scene. This **convinces** Benedick — he says they could've been "**misled**" and is the first person to **suspect Don John**.

3) The Friar suggests that they **pretend** Hero is **dead**, so that people will **mourn** her rather than focus on her **shame**. This will also give time for the **truth** to come out.

4) His plan emphasises how **helpless** Hero is as a **woman** — **playing dead** is her only hope of avoiding **public disgrace**. If her innocence **isn't proved**, Leonato will send her away to **hide** her "**wounded reputation**".

## Benedick and Beatrice admit their love

1) Everyone leaves **except** Benedick and Beatrice. Beatrice **cries** about Hero and Benedick **comforts** her — this is a very **different** type of conversation for them and it marks a **turning point** in their **relationship**.

2) Benedick says he would do **anything** for her. She says "**Kill Claudio**" — this **short**, **blunt** command **surprises** Benedick and the audience.

3) Beatrice speaks **violently** about Claudio, saying she would "**eat his heart**" **if** she were a **man**. His actions have **complicated** her feelings — she can't fully love Benedick because his **friend** has **dishonoured** her cousin.

4) This scene presents some significant **obstacles** for Benedick and Beatrice's relationship, but at least they have **admitted** their **feelings** for each other.

### Theme — Loyalty

Benedick shows loyalty to Beatrice by **staying** with her when Claudio leaves. She **challenges** his **loyalty** further when she asks him to **kill** Claudio. He has to **choose** between **love** and his **friend**.

## Scene 2 — Dogberry interrogates his prisoners

Dogberry, Verges and the Sexton (a church official) **interrogate** Borachio and Conrade. Dogberry is **incompetent**, so the Sexton **takes over**.

- This is the only scene where the Sexton has any **lines** — he is a **plot device**, **doing** and **saying** things that **help** move the **plot** along. The **excuse** for him being there is that he is **literate** and can **write**.

- He does the job **properly** and uncovers the **truth** — this lets Dogberry provide **humour** after the **seriousness** of Scene 1.

- The Sexton goes to tell Leonato what they have **discovered** and he **tells** the **audience** that Don John has "**stolen away**".

### TARGET GRADE 8-9

Some Shakespeare plays are known as 'problem plays' because they have elements of tragedy _and_ comedy. *Much Ado About Nothing* isn't a traditional problem play, but it does have elements of one — tragic scenes like Act 4, Scene 1 are combined with funny elements like the interrogation scene. Tragic moments create sympathy for characters, but also lead to bigger laughs when the tension is relieved with comedy.

## "O God, that I were a man!"

Beatrice is angry that men can make these accusations against her cousin and she can't do anything about it. If she could, she would get revenge on Claudio herself, but that's a man's role. Over to you, Benedick.

# Analysis of Act Five — Old Friends Argue

Claudio isn't the most popular guy in town right now — not one, not two, but three people want to duel him.

## Scene 1 — Leonato mourns for Hero...

*The atmosphere is very tense and uneasy in the first half of this scene.*

1) Leonato now believes Hero is **innocent**. He gives a long, **dramatic** speech in **blank verse** describing how **upset** he is.

2) Antonio tries to **comfort** him, but Leonato is still **grieving** for Hero as though she were really **dead** — he says his "**griefs cry louder**" than Antonio's words. Antonio quickly gives up and encourages him to seek **revenge**.

**Character — Leonato**

Leonato has **changed** his mind since the wedding scene. In the church, he spoke **harshly** to Hero and believed the **accusations** against her. Now he seems a **loving father**, determined to get **justice**.

3) Leonato and Antonio are both willing to **fight** Claudio, despite being **old men** against a skilled young **soldier**. This makes them look **ridiculous** — their **emotions** have taken over.

4) Don Pedro says he is "**sorry**" that Hero is dead, but that he and Claudio did the **right** thing. He still believes their accusations are **true**. He doesn't seem **genuinely sorry** — he's just trying to **avoid** a **fight**.

5) Claudio seems even **less sorry**. He is **insensitive** to Leonato, asking "**Who wrongs him?**" This seems **mocking**, as it should be **obvious** why Leonato is angry — as far as Claudio knows, Hero is **dead**.

## ... and Benedick challenges Claudio

1) Claudio and Don Pedro are **glad** to see Benedick. Their **lively** attitudes seem **inappropriate** and they **misread** how Benedick is feeling — they don't realise that he isn't in the **mood** to joke.

2) Benedick calls Claudio a "**villain**" and says he is **responsible** for Hero's **death**. Don Pedro and Claudio don't realise that he is **serious** — instead, they **tease** him about falling in **love**.

3) They reference their **jokes** and Benedick's statements from **earlier** in the play — they say they will put "**bull's horns**" on his head and make a **sign** labelling him "**Benedick, the married man**".

*In Act 1, Scene 1, Benedick said that's what they should do if he ever fell in love.*

4) Benedick challenges Claudio to a **duel**. He calls him "**boy**" as a mark of **disrespect** and says again that Claudio has "**killed a sweet and innocent lady**". Benedick is acting **honourably**, in **contrast** to the other two men.

© Photograph by Alastair Muir

**Character — Benedick**

At the start of the play, Benedick was a **joker** and **cynical** about **women**. Now he wants to restore Hero's **honour** and help the woman he **loves**.

5) Don Pedro says that Benedick seems "**earnest**" about the **challenge** and Claudio says his **love** for Beatrice has made him a **fool**. This is **ironic** — **Claudio** looks like a **fool** to the audience, not Benedick.

6) Don Pedro realises that Benedick told them **Don John** had **fled**. This hints that the play is heading towards its **resolution** — Don John is trying to **escape blame**, but the **truth** will soon come out.

---

**EXAM TIP**

## Explain how Shakespeare creates tension in this scene...

Leonato and Antonio are itching for a fight and Benedick's disgusted by his friends' behaviour. Don Pedro tries to keep everyone calm, but the audience still feels uneasy — you can cut the tension with a knife...

# Analysis of Act Five — The Truth is Revealed

Claudio and Don Pedro are finally sorry for what they did to Hero — it certainly took them long enough...

## Borachio confesses the truth...

**Shakespeare's Techniques — Language**

Dogberry brings **comedy** to an otherwise **tense** scene — his use of **language** is **confusing** and **humorous**.

1) Dogberry brings in Borachio and Conrade. He **lists** the prisoners' **crimes**, but says the same thing **six different ways** and uses a bizarre numbering system.

2) Don Pedro continues his inappropriately **cheerful** behaviour — he **mocks** Dogberry by calling him "<u>learned</u>" (educated). This is **ironic** because Dogberry is about to **reveal** the **deception** that **tricked** Don Pedro. Borachio **confesses** to the trick. He seems full of **remorse**, calling himself "<u>a villain</u>".

Photo by Reg Wilson © RSC.

4) However, the audience knows he **isn't** being completely **genuine** — Borachio **blames** Don John for everything, even though the plan was actually **his idea** in the first place.

5) The audience **questions** whether he is **really** sorry or if he is trying to **escape** a harsher punishment. Claudio and Don Pedro are **horrified** by the truth — the realisation is like "<u>poison</u>" to Claudio.

6) He remembers his **love** for Hero and calls her "<u>Sweet Hero!</u>" — yet again, he **changes** his mind **quickly**.

## ... and Leonato has a plan for Claudio

1) Leonato is **furious** with Borachio (and Don John), but he **hasn't forgiven** Don Pedro and Claudio either. He **sarcastically** calls them "<u>honourable men</u>" and says they are also **responsible** for Hero's death.

2) Don Pedro and Claudio beg for Leonato's **forgiveness**. Now that Hero's death **affects** them, they finally behave **appropriately**.

3) Leonato tells them to do three things — they must spread the **word** that Hero was **innocent** all along, they must **mourn** at her **tomb** and Claudio has to **marry** Hero's **cousin**.

**Theme — Deception and Misunderstanding**

Leonato continues **pretending** that Hero is **dead**. He **tricks** Claudio by saying he must marry Hero's 'cousin' (who **doesn't exist**). He can make Claudio and Don Pedro feel **guilty** and get some **revenge**, but still lead the plot towards its **happy ending**.

**Shakespeare's Techniques — Dramatic Irony**

The **audience knows** that Hero isn't really dead — Claudio and Don Pedro's **suffering** won't last long.

4) Claudio accepts this **punishment** in order to **redeem** himself — he wants to **save** his **reputation**. As the **romantic hero**, he must learn his **lesson** and prove to the audience that he is **worthy** of marrying Hero.

5) The scene ends with Dogberry's **comic farewell**, which **lightens the mood**. He is **rewarded** with money by Leonato — "<u>There's for thy pains</u>" — and so has done well for himself despite his **incompetence**.

## Write about Dogberry's language...

Dogberry is a right laugh and never fails to lighten a scene. While others like Benedick and Beatrice skilfully use language in their verbal battle of wits, Dogberry tries to be clever but only speaks nonsense.

# Analysis of Act Five — Claudio Mourns Hero

It's been a while since Benedick and Beatrice insulted each other, so they find the time for some jokes and sarcasm. They're having more fun than Claudio and Don Pedro, who pay their respects at Hero's fake tomb.

## Scene 2 — Benedick tries to be romantic

*Margaret's sexual jokes contrast with Benedick's poem, which represents traditional romance.*

1) Benedick tries to write a **poem** for Beatrice — this is something **expected** of a young nobleman in love.

2) Benedick isn't a typical **courtly lover** and decides he can't "**woo in festival terms**" — his love is more **real**.

3) Beatrice asks about Claudio and the **duel**, but Benedick **steers** the **conversation** back to **love**. He talks **openly** about love — he is **direct**, saying "**I will kiss thee**" and asking her why she fell in love with him.

4) Beatrice seems **cautious** — in Act 2, Scene 1, she hinted that she had been **hurt** by Benedick in the past. She **mocks** him and declares she will "**depart unkissed**", but her teasing doesn't seem as **bitter** as before.

5) They agree that "**suffer love**" is a good phrase to describe their relationship. Benedick jokes that he loves Beatrice **against his will**. They are **self-aware** — they both seem to know that their relationship isn't a **typical romance**.

6) The scene ends as Ursula **tells** Benedick and Beatrice about Don John's **plot**. This **structure** lets Beatrice **move on** towards a **happy ending** — no longer **angry** with Claudio, she can start **loving** Benedick.

**TARGET GRADE 8-9**

Benedick briefly tries to be a courtly lover, but his final words in this scene are quite ordinary. After a list of exaggerated romantic actions, he finishes: "I will go with thee to thy uncle's." This is an example of 'bathos' — an anticlimax created when poetic language is followed by something ordinary. The sudden change in tone adds humour to the end of the scene.

## Scene 3 — Claudio mourns at Hero's tomb

1) Claudio and Don Pedro visit the **tomb** where Hero is '**buried**'. The mood is very **solemn** — the scene takes place at **night** and the stage is lit by **torches**.

*An epitaph is something written in memory of someone who has died.*

2) Claudio's **epitaph** for Hero acknowledges her **wrongful** death and shows his **grief**. The men are **respectful** as they carry out the mourning **ceremony**.

© Photograph by Alastair Muir

**Shakespeare's Techniques — Poetry and Prose**

Claudio and Don Pedro speak in **verse** in this scene. This includes **rhyming couplets** such as "**So the life that died with shame / Lives in death with glorious fame.**" This shows their **sombre** mood and the **formal** nature of the mourning **ceremony**.

3) Claudio is **worried** about his wedding to Hero's '**cousin**'. He appeals to Hymen, the ancient Greek **god of marriage**, and hopes that this wedding won't end in **tragedy** like the last one.

4) The **audience** is confident that it won't be tragic — Claudio will soon be **celebrating** instead of **mourning**. This scene comes **just before** the **final** scene of the play — it wraps up the **tragic** elements of the story and allows the next scene to focus on the **happy ending**.

**KEY QUOTE**

## "Thou and I are too wise to woo peaceably."

Benedick and Beatrice are bickering again — looks like some things never change. But they're not just throwing insults around to show how clever they are — this time it's about their love for each other.

# Analysis of Act Five — Hero is Alive

The play moves from a tomb to a church, which is a tiny hint that the happy ending is finally in sight. Everyone's alive and in love, and the bad guy gets caught — everything is wrapped up nicely.

## Scene 4 — Claudio meets Hero's 'cousin'...

1) Leonato puts the final step of his **plan** in motion — he sends Hero and the rest of the women offstage to put on **masks** so that Claudio can be tricked.

2) Benedick tells Leonato that he **loves** Beatrice and she feels the same. He asks the Friar to **marry** them.

3) Benedick is glad he doesn't have to **duel** Claudio, but there is still **tension** between the two of them.

**Shakespeare's Techniques — Puns and Wordplay**

Claudio makes more jokes about **horns** and **cuckolds**. In Act 1, Scene 1, Don Pedro said that eventually a "<u>savage bull</u>" could be **tamed** — Claudio now reminds Benedick that they joked about this "<u>savage bull</u>" and mocks him for **changing** his mind about **marriage**.

4) Don Pedro comments that Benedick has a "<u>February face</u>" (he looks **serious**). This could suggest that Benedick is **nervous** about getting **married**.

5) Claudio isn't allowed to see his bride's **face**, but he is **committed** to getting married and **making up** for his actions. He is **rewarded** for this — once he **swears** to marry her, Hero **removes** her **mask**.

6) Hero and Leonato use **imagery** of **life** and **death** to explain the plan. She had to be '**dead**' to escape the **lies** and she can '**live**' again now that the **truth** is out.

## ... and Benedick proposes to Beatrice

1) Benedick and Beatrice are **reluctant** to **publicly** admit their feelings. They say they **love** each other "<u>no more than reason</u>". They still don't know that their friends **tricked** them into falling in love.

2) Claudio and Hero produce **love poems** written by Benedick and Beatrice to **prove** that they really do love each other. Benedick and Beatrice still **bicker** and **tease** each other until finally he **kisses** her.

3) Benedick tells Don Pedro to find himself a **wife**. In Act 1, Scene 1, Benedick was **horrified** that men "<u>turn husband</u>", but now he **encourages** his friend to do it.

4) A messenger announces that Don John has been **captured**. This **conveniently** resolves the **final issue** of the play — the audience are now confident that **justice** will be done.

5) Benedick says they'll deal with Don John later — now it's time for **dancing** and **music**.

**Shakespeare's Techniques — Form**

This is a **comedy**, so everything is **resolved** at the end — the music and dancing **symbolises** this. However, the audience may **question** how **successful** the relationships will be. It's unclear if Claudio and Hero are well-suited, or if Benedick and Beatrice's "<u>merry war</u>" will become a **happy marriage**.

 ## "One Hero died defiled, but I do live"

Hero doesn't get much to say in this final scene, but at least everyone knows she was innocent all along. Hopefully she and Claudio can have a fresh start — assuming he doesn't change his mind yet again...

# Practice Questions

Let's check what happens when, who's in love with who, and why the characters keep tricking each other.

## Quick Questions

1) Which characters arrive in Messina at the start of the play?

2) Who does Don Pedro pretend to be at the masked ball?

For even more practice, try the Much Ado About Nothing Sudden Fail Quiz — just scan this QR code!

**Sudden Fail Quiz**

3) Describe how Benedick is tricked into falling in love with Beatrice.

4) Who do the Watch arrest?

5) How does Leonato initially react to Claudio's accusations against Hero?

6) What does Beatrice ask Benedick to do after he admits to her that he loves her?

7) Who helps Dogberry and Verges interrogate their prisoners?

Finally, a useful chief of the Watch!

8) Who does Claudio think he is going to marry at the end of the play?

9) What do Claudio and Hero use to prove that Benedick and Beatrice love each other?

## In-depth Questions

1) Using examples from the play, describe the atmosphere during the masked ball.

2) Describe the similarities between the tricks in Act 2, Scene 3 and Act 3, Scene 1.

3) Do you think that Don Pedro is happy to remain unmarried?  Explain your answer.

4) Choose an example of a misunderstanding and explain how it drives the plot of the play.

5) Do you think that the audience is supposed to like or dislike Claudio?
   Use examples from the play to support your answer.

## Target Grade 8-9

1) Lower-status characters play an important role in uncovering Borachio's plot.  Do you find the portrayal of lower-status characters to be positive?  Explain your answer.

2) Some audiences find Benedick and Beatrice's switch from opponents to lovers too abrupt.  Do you agree with this?  Give evidence for your answer.

# Practice Questions

Let's step it up a notch with some exam-style questions. These might look a bit tricky, but they're important —
they'll test how well you know the play and also help you practise the kind of task you'll face in the exam.

## Exam-style Questions

1) How does Shakespeare present Benedick and Beatrice's relationship?
   Refer to the extract below from Act 2, Scene 1 and to the play as a whole.

   | | |
   |---|---|
   | **Beatrice:** | Will you not tell me who told you so? |
   | **Benedick:** | No, you shall pardon me. |
   | **Beatrice:** | Nor will you not tell me who you are? |
   | **Benedick:** | Not now. |
   | **Beatrice:** | That I was disdainful, and that I had my good wit out of the *Hundred Merry Tales* — well, this was Signior Benedick that said so. |
   | **Benedick:** | What's he? |
   | **Beatrice:** | I am sure you know him well enough. |
   | **Benedick:** | Not I, believe me. |
   | **Beatrice:** | Did he never make you laugh? |
   | **Benedick:** | I pray you, what is he? |
   | **Beatrice:** | Why, he is the Prince's jester, a very dull fool. Only his gift is in devising impossible slanders. None but libertines delight in him, and the commendation is not in his wit, but in his villainy, for he both pleases men and angers them, and then they laugh at him and beat him. I am sure he is in the fleet. I would he had boarded me. |
   | **Benedick:** | When I know the gentleman, I'll tell him what you say. |
   | **Beatrice:** | Do, do. He'll but break a comparison or two on me, which, peradventure not marked or not laughed at, strikes him into melancholy, and then there's a partridge wing saved, for the fool will eat no supper that night. |

   (Act 2, Scene 1)

2) How does Shakespeare present Don John as the villain in the play?
   Refer to at least two different parts of the play in your answer.

3) Read Act 5, Scene 1 from **"Tush, tush, man"** to **"Nay, as I am a gentleman, I will."**

   a) How is Leonato presented in this extract?

   b) In this extract, Leonato and Antonio both defend their honour by challenging Claudio
      to a duel. What is the significance of honour elsewhere in the play?
      You should consider:
      • times when honour is important
      • how honour affects characters' actions.

# Character Profile — Hero

Hero isn't a big talker and mostly gets pushed around by the other characters. You still need to know all about her though — she might not do much, but she manages to be pretty central to the plot of the play.

## Hero is pure and innocent

1) Hero is Leonato's "<u>only heir</u>" — she will **inherit** all his **property**, which makes her an **attractive prospect** for men to marry.

2) Hero represents the **ideal** Elizabethan woman — **quiet**, **beautiful** and **honourable**. Claudio describes her as "<u>the sweetest lady that ever I looked on</u>".

**Hero is...**

submissive: "<u>It is my cousin's duty to make curtsy</u>"

playful: "<u>So angle we for Beatrice</u>"

pure: "<u>a modest young lady</u>"

3) At the end of the play, her **honour** is **restored** and she confirms her **innocence** — "<u>I do live, / And surely as I live, I am a maid</u>." She ends the play as she started it — a **pure** and **dutiful** woman.

## Her fate is controlled by the male characters

1) As a typical **Elizabethan woman**, Hero is expected to be **obedient** to her **father** or **husband**. Unlike Beatrice, she is **submissive** to men and **doesn't speak** much.

2) She's often referred to as a **possession** — Claudio calls her "<u>a jewel</u>" and a "<u>precious gift</u>".

3) Hero is **rejected** by the male characters who believe she's been **unfaithful**. Claudio tells Leonato, "<u>Give not this rotten orange to your friend</u>" and refuses to marry her.

© Sam Goldwyn / Renaissance / BBC / Kobal / REX / Shutterstock

**Shakespeare's Techniques — Imagery**

Leonato uses a **metaphor** to suggest that Hero's **reputation** is damaged forever — "<u>O, she is fallen / Into a pit of ink</u>". This suggests she's **stained** and will **never** be **morally clean** again.

4) Leonato thinks that Hero has **shamed** him with her behaviour.

5) She exclaims "<u>O, God defend me, how am I beset!</u>" which suggests she feels **powerless** to help herself.

6) Even when Hero is proved innocent, this is **achieved** by **male** characters — Hero only plays a **small role** in the **Friar's plan** to restore her reputation. She might seem **passive** or **weak** to a **modern audience**.

## She is also light-hearted and playful

There is also a **different**, more **mischievous** side to Hero. She often shows this when she's with the other **female characters**:

- She **enjoys** working with Margaret and Ursula to **trick** Beatrice — "<u>No truly, Ursula, she is too disdainful</u>".

- She **insults** Beatrice as part of the trick — "<u>Disdain and scorn ride sparkling in her eyes</u>".

- She proves that Beatrice loves Benedick by producing a **love poem** that she's **stolen** from Beatrice's **pocket**.

**TARGET GRADE 8-9**

Claudio doesn't see Hero's playful side — in fact, he doesn't know much about her personality at all. This makes it seem ironic when he criticises her at the wedding for being "but the sign and semblance of her honour" (looking honourable but being corrupt) — it's the first time he has paid attention to Hero's personality. It seems like he only cares about her personality when it might damage her (and his own) reputation.

**KEY QUOTE**

## "And seemed I ever otherwise to you?"

Hero knows she's been completely faithful to Claudio, so she has no idea why he'd think anything else. She's exactly as pure and honest as she seems, but it doesn't take much to convince people she's a liar.

# Character Profile — Claudio

What to say about Claudio? This guy falls for any old trick and is pretty fickle about his feelings for Hero.

## Claudio is a respected soldier...

1) Claudio returns from war as a **hero** — he has achieved "<u>the feats of a lion</u>". As a result, Don Pedro has "<u>bestowed much honour</u>" on him.

2) Claudio falls **madly** in **love** with Hero and his **identity** quickly shifts from a **soldier** to a typical **courtly lover**. Leonato is happy to marry her to a **respected** man and the **wedding** is quickly arranged.

3) However, **not everybody** respects Claudio. Don John is **bitter** about being **defeated** in the war and wants **revenge** on Claudio — "<u>that young start-up hath all the glory of my overthrow</u>".

### Claudio is...

jealous: "<u>civil as an orange, and something of that jealous complexion</u>"

eager: "<u>time goes on crutches till love have all his rites.</u>"

immature: "<u>We had like to have had our two noses snapped off with two old men without teeth.</u>"

## ... but he is easily influenced

1) Claudio is **instantly** attracted to Hero, but he seeks **reassurance** from his friends Benedick and Don Pedro that she is "<u>worthy</u>".

2) He **looks up** to Don Pedro and **follows** his lead. Don Pedro is a **prince** and **social status** is important to Claudio as an **ambitious** count.

### Context

Claudio is a **rich young count** — this makes him an **attractive suitor** for Hero. An Elizabethan audience would recognise him as a **romantic hero** — a man who falls in love **quickly** and thinks his love interest is **perfect** without knowing her very well.

3) Claudio can be **quick** to **doubt** his **friends**. He's **jealous** of Don Pedro at the masked ball and believes he has **betrayed** him.

4) He quickly **believes** Don John's **lies**. This makes him seem **suspicious** and **foolish** to a **modern** audience, but an **Elizabethan** audience may have **understood** his desire to protect his **honour**.

## He isn't a perfect romantic hero

1) Claudio's **feelings** change very **quickly** and don't always seem **genuine**.

2) Shakespeare suggests that Claudio is interested in Hero's **money** and **status**. When he asks "<u>hath Leonato any son, my lord?</u>", he is trying to find out how much Hero will **inherit** from her father.

3) Claudio doesn't always act **honourably**. He is **cruel** to Hero by **publicly shaming** her and he **doesn't** initially **grieve** for her when she 'dies'.

4) He doesn't admit when he's **wrong**. After Hero is proved **innocent**, he still claims "<u>yet sinned I not</u>" and that he was **right** to defend his **honour**. This makes the audience **question** whether he **deserves** to marry Hero.

5) However, Claudio eventually **regrets** what he has done and begs for Leonato's **forgiveness**. Only then can he and Hero get **married**.

© Geraint Lewis / Alamy Stock Photo

### KEY QUOTE

## "where I should wed, there will I shame her."

Claudio thinks he's an honourable chap, but he humiliates Hero at their first wedding and proves his reputation is more important to him than love. Definitely not someone to take relationship tips from.

28

# Character Profile — Beatrice

Beatrice and Hero might be related, but they couldn't be more different. Beatrice has no time for controlling men or gender stereotypes. She speaks her mind and gets some of the best lines in the play (if you ask me).

## Beatrice is outspoken and confident...

1) Beatrice provides a clear **contrast** to her cousin, Hero. While Hero is quiet and submissive, Beatrice has a similar number of **lines** to the **male** characters and gives her opinion **confidently**.

2) She is **witty**, **intelligent** and **playful** — she uses lots of **wordplay** and **puns** in her speech and isn't afraid to **answer back** to the men.

**Beatrice is...**

free-spirited: "I know her spirits are as coy and wild / As haggards of the rock."

witty: "she mocks all her wooers out of suit."

frustrated: "O God, that I were a man!"

**Context**

Beatrice goes against traditional **stereotypes** about **women** in Shakespeare's time — she is **outspoken**, **independent** and initially **refuses** to get **married**.

3) Beatrice is **determined** — she isn't interested in **marriage** at the beginning of the play and **doesn't** let her family's **criticism** of her **change her mind**.

4) She claims in Act 1, Scene 1 that she'd "rather hear my dog bark at a crow than a man swear he loves me". It's **ironic** when she does then **fall in love**.

## ... but she has a sensitive side

© Donald Cooper / photostage

1) Shakespeare suggests that Beatrice has been **hurt** by Benedick in the **past** and so she is **cautious** about their relationship. Beatrice tells Don Pedro that Benedick once **won** her heart with "false dice".

2) Beatrice is **loyal** and **defends** Hero completely, saying "She is wronged, she is slandered".

3) She has a **vulnerable** side — when she overhears Ursula and Hero speaking about her "pride and scorn", she **reflects** on their **criticism** and decides to **change** her attitude towards Benedick.

## She changes her mind about love and marriage

1) At the **start** of the play, Beatrice says she **prays** that God will "send me no husband". She knows marriage is **expected** of her, but it isn't what she **wants**.

**Shakespeare's Techniques — Language**

Beatrice and Benedick frequently share conversations **equally**, speaking **alternate lines**. Shakespeare does this to show their close **connection**.

2) However, Shakespeare shows Beatrice **cares** about Benedick — her **first line** in the play asks if he has "returned from the wars".

3) Beatrice and Benedick enjoy their "skirmish of wit" — they are **equally matched** and can **joke** with each other. They grow **closer** over the course of the play and their conversations become more **intimate**.

4) By the **end** of the play, she has **changed** her mind about marriage and about Benedick. She declares she **loves** him "with so much of my heart that none is left to protest".

### "I was born to speak all mirth and no matter."

Beatrice knows she's clever and isn't afraid to show it. She enjoys outwitting people in conversations and shocking people with what she says. There's only one person who is a match for her — he's up next...

Section Three — Characters

# Character Profile — Benedick

Benedick is a joker and likes a good laugh. He isn't keen on romance, but all of that changes when he finally realises that he and Beatrice are made for each other. It doesn't take a genius to work that one out...

## Benedick is outspoken and confident...

> A 'cynical' person is often pessimistic and doesn't believe in romantic or idealistic approaches to life.

1) Benedick is **popular** and **self-assured** — he claims to be "<u>loved of all ladies</u>" and he is **respected** by the other characters as "<u>a very proper man</u>".

2) He makes a lot of **jokes** — these are often about **women** because he **doesn't trust** them.

3) Benedick is very **similar** to Beatrice. However, as a **man**, Benedick is in a much **stronger position** in society. When Hero is slandered, Beatrice asks Benedick to **help** her, telling him to "<u>kill Claudio</u>".

**Benedick is...**

cynical: "<u>Shall I never see a bachelor of three-score again?</u>"

honourable: "<u>he is of a noble strain, of approved valour and confirmed honesty</u>"

reflective: "<u>Thou and I are too wise to woo peaceably.</u>"

4) Benedick **contrasts** with Claudio — Claudio is naive, easily manipulated and conventional in his approach to love. Benedick is more **independent** and **cynical**.

> See p.39 for more on Benedick and Claudio's attitudes to courtly love.

## ... but he has a sensitive side

1) In Act 1, Benedick reveals that he thinks Beatrice is **prettier** than Hero. He says she "<u>exceeds her as much in beauty as the first of May doth the last of December</u>".

2) He takes Beatrice's **insults** seriously — he claims "<u>every word stabs</u>" and that it's like "<u>a whole army shooting</u>" at him. Despite Benedick's **confidence**, he is **vulnerable** and wants Beatrice to like him.

3) Benedick **supports** Beatrice — he agrees to **duel** Claudio and puts her before his **loyalty** to his friend.

© AF archive / Alamy Stock Photo

4) Claudio and Don Pedro often look to Benedick for **entertainment**, but after Hero is **shamed**, he **refuses** to joke with them. He seems more **sensitive** than the others, who don't even **realise** he's **angry** with them.

## He changes his mind about love and marriage

1) Benedick **doesn't trust** women and says he will **never** fall in love. He tells Claudio and Don Pedro "<u>if I do, hang me in a bottle like a cat and shoot at me</u>".

2) Later in the play, he realises that his **feelings** have **changed** — "<u>but doth not the appetite alter?</u>" He becomes much less interested in joking about marriage with the other men.

**Shakespeare's Techniques — Language**

After his friends trick him, Benedick is the **only character** on stage — this allows Shakespeare to reveal his **inner thoughts** in a **soliloquy**. His speech is more **honest**, since he is not in the presence of **other characters**.

3) Benedick **changes** his mind about Beatrice — he initially calls her "<u>Lady Disdain</u>" but later declares he is "<u>horribly in love with her</u>". This **mirrors** Beatrice's **change of heart** and shows how **similar** they are.

---

**EXAM TIP**

## Discuss how Benedick changes throughout the play...

Benedick starts off as a cynic who can't imagine anything worse than getting married. His opinions and behaviour change as he realises that love might not be so bad after all — everyone say *awww*...

---

**Section Three — Characters**

# Character Profile — Don Pedro

Don Pedro doesn't have any relationship drama himself, but he gets really involved in other people's love lives. If you get confused between Don Pedro and his brother, Don Pedro is (mostly) the nice one.

## Don Pedro is a powerful man

1) Don Pedro is a **prince** and therefore has the **highest status** among the characters. He is **influential** — the others **listen** to him and **follow** him.

2) He is widely **respected** — Leonato welcomes him **warmly** and seems **pleased** to have him as a guest. The characters often address him **politely**, calling him "**your grace**".

3) Claudio looks to him for **advice** and Don Pedro is happy to **help** — "**my love is thine to teach**".

4) Don Pedro **contrasts** with his **illegitimate** brother Don John — they've recently **fought** on **opposing** sides. Don Pedro wants to be "**reconciled**", but Don John is only interested in causing **trouble** for his brother.

> **Don Pedro is...**
> powerful: "**I charge thee on thy allegiance.**"
> loyal: "**Claudio, I have wooed in thy name**"
> calm: "**Nay, do not quarrel with us**"

*Shakespeare uses lots of opposites in the play — this technique is called antithesis. See p.54 for more.*

## He encourages the romantic partnerships...

1) Don Pedro confidently **takes charge** of the **plan** to woo Hero — he tells Claudio "**thou shalt have her**" and "**I will fit thee with the remedy**". He is **loyal** to his friend and uses his **influence** and **status** to **help** him.

> **Shakespeare's Techniques — Imagery**
>
> Don Pedro uses **images** of **capture** when uniting the couples, such as a "**net**" and taking Hero "**prisoner**". These reinforce the idea that he is **controlling** the action. He also calls the tricks a "**sport**", suggesting he **enjoys** the **challenge**.

2) Don Pedro also **suggests** the plan that **unites** Beatrice and Benedick — he **enjoys** playing tricks and is **good** at it. Act 2, Scene 1 ends with him **explaining** his **idea** to the others and starting to **plan** the **trick** in more detail.

3) He is an **observer** of love, rather than participating in romance himself. He does show affection to Beatrice, but **doesn't pursue** her when she **rejects** him for being "**too costly**".

## ... but he also makes mistakes

1) Don Pedro is **taken in** by Don John's **trick**. He chooses to "**disgrace**" Hero with Claudio, which shows he **doesn't** always act **wisely**. This also **influences** Leonato to turn against his daughter.

2) He is **blinded** by his belief in the importance of **reputation** — he is **fooled** by Don John's **deception** because he wants to **protect** Claudio's **reputation** as well as his **own**.

© Photo 12 / Alamy Stock Photo

3) However, he **admits** that he has made a **mistake** about Hero. He is truly **sorry** and will "**bend under any heavy weight**" to make it up to Leonato. Don Pedro is **honest**, **fair** and wants to make things **right**.

---

**Mention deception when writing about Don Pedro...**

Don Pedro thinks he's the master of sneaky plans, but he doesn't manage to avoid being deceived himself. He enjoys playing tricks on his friends, but he also falls for Don John's lies and believes that Hero is dead.

# Character Profile — Don John

Now for the play's other Don — he's a nasty piece of work who causes a right mess for everyone else...

## Don John is cruel and manipulative

1) Don John is the "__plain-dealing villain__" of the play — he **dislikes** the other characters and wants to cause **problems** for them. He is responsible for the plot to **ruin** Hero's **reputation** and her **relationship**.

2) He **disappears** from Messina when Claudio rejects Hero. He has "__secretly stolen away__", suggesting he's trying to **escape blame**.

3) He doesn't get away with his **crimes** — he's **brought back** at the end of the play by **armed men** to face "__brave punishments__".

**Don John is...**

miserable: "__of a very melancholy disposition.__"

sly: "__Be cunning in the working__"

malicious: "__to despite them, I will endeavour any thing__."

**TARGET GRADE** (8-9)

Even tiny details like pronouns can be revealing. In Act 1, Scene 3, Don John is shown to be selfish through his use of the first-person pronoun 'I': "I cannot hide what I am — I must be sad when I have cause...". He uses it 8 times in this line alone.

## He's an outsider

1) Don John is **illegitimate** — he was born **outside** of **marriage**. Like most illegitimate Elizabethans, he has **no rights** to his father's **inheritance** and doesn't have a **proper place** within the family.

2) He has a **difficult** relationship with his **brother**, Don Pedro — before the start of the play, they **fought** on **opposite sides** in the **war**.

3) Don John feels like Don Pedro **controls** and **restricts** him. He claims that "__if I had my liberty, I would do my liking__".

4) The other characters **don't like** or **trust** him:

- Benedick claims his "__spirits toil in frame of villainies__".

- Borachio describes him as "__the devil my master__".

- Don Pedro accuses him of being "__framed of treachery__" — this suggests he is **untrustworthy** and **unreliable**.

- Don John thinks that everyone else is **happy** about his defeat — "__their cheer is the greater that I am subdued__".

© Photograph by Alastair Muir

## He's not a very good villain

1) Don John **accepts** he is a **villain**. He says "__it better fits my blood to be disdained of all__" — this shows he's **aware** that people don't like him.

2) However, he isn't a very **successful** villain. His first plan quickly **fails** and then the second plan to disgrace Hero is **thought up** by Borachio.

3) He isn't a **complex** villain — he's there to **cause trouble** and further the **plot**. He **disappears** from the play once he has served his **purpose**. This is a **comedy**, so the villain has to **fail**.

**Shakespeare's Techniques — Dramatic Irony**

The **audience** observes Don John's cunning plans, but most of the other **characters** are **unaware** of these plots. This makes the action more **exciting** as the audience is **waiting** for the characters to find out the truth.

**KEY QUOTE** — "Will it serve for any model to build mischief on?"

Don John makes it clear from the start that he wants to cause chaos and leaps at any chance he gets. Too bad for him that he's not great at plotting — he'd be an even worse villain without Borachio to help him...

Section Three — Characters

# Character Profile — Leonato

Leonato's meant to be mature and sensible, but he still makes mistakes and plays tricks with the best of them.

## Leonato is the well-respected governor of Messina

1) Leonato is an **important** public figure, but in the play he is mostly concerned with **family** matters.

2) He is **father** to Hero, **brother** to Antonio, **uncle** to Beatrice and **host** to Don Pedro and his men. He is **generous** and seems to **enjoy** hosting his **guests**.

3) Leonato is **respected** by other characters. Benedick says he doesn't believe Leonato would **lie**, which makes him **believe** the **trick** his friends play on him.

4) Leonato is one of the most **mature** characters and this is reflected in the way he **talks** — most of his speech is **formal** and **polite**. He often speaks in **verse** and uses lots of **imagery**.

**Leonato is...**

respected: "<u>Knavery cannot, sure, hide himself in such reverence.</u>"
impatient: "<u>Come, Friar Francis, be brief.</u>"
protective: "<u>thou hast belied mine innocent child.</u>"

## He is a dutiful Elizabethan father...

© Manuel Harlan

1) Leonato represents the traditional, **patriarchal** society. He has strict **expectations** of Hero.

See p.42 for more on gender.

2) He **instructs** Hero how to **behave** ("<u>I charge thee do so, as thou art my child</u>") and Antonio trusts she will be "<u>ruled</u>" by Leonato.

**Theme — Gender**

**Unmarried women** were expected to **obey** their **fathers** completely. It's **unsurprising** that Hero does not **question** Leonato's **authority**.

3) However, Leonato clearly **loves** his daughter and wants the **best** for her. He is **old** and wants to know that Hero will be **provided for** in the future. In Elizabethan society, this meant she had to make a **good marriage**.

4) He is happy for her to marry **either** Claudio or Don Pedro, but whoever **proposes** to her, she must **accept** — "<u>you know your answer</u>".

## ... but he can also be foolish

1) Leonato **believes** the word of the **male characters** who accuse Hero. He asks "<u>would the two princes lie</u>" and **rejects** her at the wedding.

2) He is **horrified** by the accusations and acts **rashly**, saying Hero would be better off **dead** — "<u>death is the fairest cover for her shame</u>". He's more **concerned** about his **reputation** (see p.37) than his daughter.

**Theme — Honour and Reputation**

Leonato and Antonio are both willing to **fight** to defend Hero's **honour** — even though **neither** of them could **defeat** Claudio. They believe their **family's reputation** is worth **dying** for.

3) Leonato makes himself look **ridiculous** by challenging Claudio to a **duel**. He has **no chance** of winning — even he acknowledges his "<u>grey hairs and bruise of many days</u>". He is so **angry** that he doesn't **care**.

4) A **modern** audience might find it **strange** that Leonato is **happy** for Hero to marry Claudio after the way he **treated** her. Claudio is still a **respected nobleman** — that's what matters to Leonato.

**KEY QUOTE**

## "Thou hast so wronged mine innocent child and me"

Leonato is a family man, but he's also worried about his reputation and it takes him a while to believe that Hero is innocent. Once he does, he's determined to defend her and to make Claudio feel guilty.

# Character Profile — Dogberry

Poor Dogberry — he's rubbish at his job and no one takes him seriously. At least he's pleased with himself...

## Dogberry is a useless constable

1) Dogberry and Verges (his deputy) are officers of the **Watch** (see p.16) — their job is to keep the **peace** in Messina.

2) He is **incompetent** — he advises the Watch to let thieves "<u>steal out of your company</u>" and allows them to **fall asleep** on the job.

3) He frequently **bickers** with Verges, who is just as **incompetent**.

4) He has a **low social status** and is a "<u>poor man</u>". His **incompetence** means that he isn't taken **seriously**:

> **Dogberry is...**
>
> sincere: "<u>be vigitant, I beseech you</u>"
>
> self-important: "<u>I am a wise fellow, and, which is more, an officer</u>"
>
> incompetent: "<u>Master Constable, you go not the way to examine.</u>"

- Leonato calls him "<u>tedious</u>" because he **babbles** while trying to explain that he has **arrested** two prisoners.

- Don Pedro **mocks** his **repetitive** and **confused** speech, sarcastically calling him "<u>learned constable</u>".

## Shakespeare uses him to provide comic relief

1) Dogberry pretends to be **clever** and attempts to use **long words** that he **doesn't understand** — "<u>we are now to examination these men</u>". He tries to **copy** the poetic style of **high-status** men like Leonato and Don Pedro.

2) He sees himself as **respectable** and **serious**, so he's **outraged** when Conrade calls him "<u>an ass</u>". The audience would find his **false pride** amusing.

> **Shakespeare's Techniques — Language**
>
> Dogberry uses lots of **malapropisms** in his speech — he uses a **wrong word** that **sounds like** the one he **means**. For example, he says "<u>odorous</u>" ('smelly') instead of "<u>odious</u>" ('hateful'). He often ends up speaking **nonsense**, which has a **comic effect**.

## He is more honest than the noble characters

© Donald Cooper / photostage

1) Unlike the **noble** characters, Dogberry **doesn't** try to **deceive** anyone or act behind anyone's back.

2) Even though he is **bad** at his **job** and **struggles** to **communicate**, he works to bring about the **truth**. The **high-status** characters don't always do this.

3) Dogberry and the Watch are key in **discovering** Don John's **plot** — they **stop** the **tragic events** and direct the play towards its **happy ending**.

> **Shakespeare's Techniques — Dramatic Irony**
>
> The audience knows that the Watch have discovered Don John's plot, which makes it frustrating when Leonato dismisses Dogberry and Verges before the **wedding**.

4) Borachio tells Don Pedro that "<u>what your wisdoms could not discover, these shallow fools have brought to light</u>". Shakespeare may be **standing up** for people of **low status** and suggesting they shouldn't be ignored.

---

**EXAM TIP**

## Write about Dogberry as a comic character...

Dogberry has a way with words, but not in the same way that Benedick and Beatrice do... He provides a different type of humour — he's comic because of his **incompetence** rather than his **intelligence** and **wit**.

# Character Profile — Other Characters

That's all the main characters in the play, but there are a few minor characters you should know about too.

## Margaret and Ursula are Hero's serving women

1) Margaret adds **comic relief** to the play. She often makes **sexual jokes** — before the wedding, she tells Hero that she will be "<u>heavier soon by the weight of a man</u>."

2) As a **servant**, it's **less shocking** for Margaret to refer to sex. She **contrasts** with Hero, who is from a **noble family** and is expected to be **pure** and **innocent** — Hero thinks Margaret should be "<u>ashamed</u>" of her jokes.

3) Ursula plays an important role in **tricking** Beatrice. Hero wouldn't have spoken **openly** and **honestly** about Beatrice with the **male** characters — the serving women allow her to **speak her mind**.

© Photograph by Alastair Muir

### Theme — Deception and Misunderstanding

Margaret is **tricked** into playing a role in Don John's **plot** — she is easily **taken advantage** of by the **male** characters. Borachio **defends** her as "<u>just and virtuous</u>" and Leonato concludes she took part "<u>against her will</u>".

## Borachio and Conrade are Don John's companions

1) Borachio is a **clever** and **persuasive** villain. He brings Don John the **news** that Claudio loves Hero, and thinks up a **plan** to "<u>misuse the prince, to vex Claudio, to undo Hero and kill Leonato</u>".

2) Borachio **manipulates** Don John. He earns **money** ("<u>a thousand ducats</u>") for tricking Claudio, but he **shifts** the **blame** when he is arrested, claiming Don John "<u>incensed me to slander</u>".

### Shakespeare's Techniques — Language

Borachio uses **imperatives** (commanding verbs) to **instruct** Don John. He tells him to "<u>Go</u>", "<u>tell them</u>" and "<u>be you constant in the accusation</u>". This highlights Borachio's **central role** in the plan to shame Hero.

3) However, Borachio is also **proud** and **careless** — he **boasts** about arranging the deception and being paid for it. This **leads** to the **failure** of the plan and Don John's **arrest**.

4) Borachio and Conrade **escape blame** — Borachio admits he is the "<u>wronger</u>", but ultimately Don John is **accused** as "<u>the author</u>" of the plot.

## The Friar is a voice of reason

1) Friar Francis **defends** Hero after she is **accused** (**unlike** most of the **male** characters). He is convinced there is a "<u>biting error</u>" and correctly guesses that Hero is "<u>guiltless</u>".

2) He suggests the **plan** to **pretend** that Hero is **dead**. It is **ironic** that a **religious** figure would encourage **deception**, but his plan does bring about the play's **happy ending**.

3) The other characters **listen** to the Friar — he has **religious authority** and is **respected**. He tells Leonato to "<u>let my counsel sway you</u>" and Leonato **agrees** to his plan.

**TARGET GRADE 8-9**

In Elizabethan times, friars took a vow of poverty and survived on charity. Despite this, they still held authority — this can be seen in the Friar's use of imperatives in Act 4, Scene 1. Commands such as "hear me", "call me" and "pause awhile" show that he wields authority over the noble characters in the play, despite his lack of wealth.

**EXAM TIP**

## Mentioning minor characters will impress the examiner...

The minor characters aren't always at the centre of the action, but they still have an important role in the various plots and plans that take place. Make sure you understand what their purpose is in the play.

# Practice Questions

These questions will make sure you know who's who in the play. You'll be a total expert in no time.

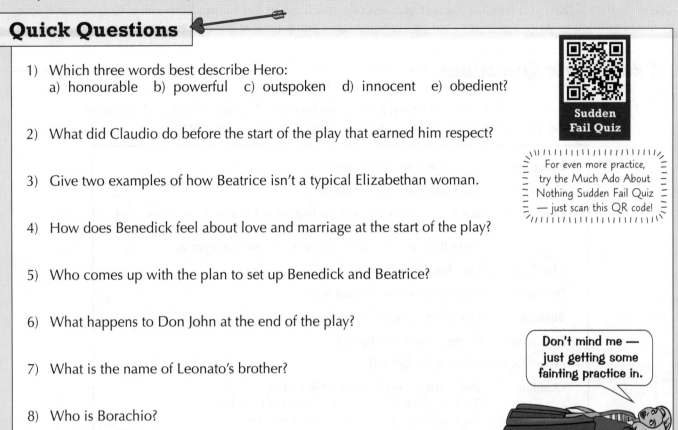

## Quick Questions

1) Which three words best describe Hero:
   a) honourable   b) powerful   c) outspoken   d) innocent   e) obedient?

2) What did Claudio do before the start of the play that earned him respect?

3) Give two examples of how Beatrice isn't a typical Elizabethan woman.

4) How does Benedick feel about love and marriage at the start of the play?

5) Who comes up with the plan to set up Benedick and Beatrice?

6) What happens to Don John at the end of the play?

7) What is the name of Leonato's brother?

8) Who is Borachio?

**Sudden Fail Quiz**

For even more practice, try the Much Ado About Nothing Sudden Fail Quiz — just scan this QR code!

Don't mind me — just getting some fainting practice in.

## In-depth Questions

1) How much is Hero's personality shaped by expectations of women in Elizabethan society? Find evidence from the play to back up your answer.

2) Do you think Claudio really loves Hero? Explain your answer.

3) Describe Beatrice's opposition to marriage and how she changes over the course of the play.

4) How does Benedick's character contrast with Claudio's? Give some examples from the play.

5) Do you think that Leonato is a good father? Use examples to explain your answer.

## Target Grade 8-9

1) Don John and Don Pedro both enjoy tricking others. Explore the similarities and differences in their deceptive behaviour.

2) Explain whether you consider the Friar to be a three-dimensional character or simply a plot device.

# Practice Questions

Now for some lovely exam-style questions. 'Lovely' might not be quite the right word, but they're definitely useful — they'll help you practise the sort of questions you'll get in the exam. Remember to take some time at the beginning to write a plan for your answer and leave some time at the end to check through your work.

## Exam-style Questions

1) How does Shakespeare use the character of Claudio to explore the theme of deception? Refer to the extract below from Act 2, Scene 1 and to the play as a whole.

| | |
|---|---|
| **Don John:** | Are not you Signior Benedick? |
| **Claudio:** | You know me well — I am he. |
| **Don John:** | Signior, you are very near my brother in his love; he is enamoured on Hero. I pray you, dissuade him from her; she is no equal for his birth — you may do the part of an honest man in it. |
| **Claudio:** | How know you he loves her? |
| **Don John:** | I heard him swear his affection. |
| **Borachio:** | So did I too, and he swore he would marry her tonight. |
| **Don John:** | Come, let us to the banquet. |

*Exeunt* DON JOHN *and* BORACHIO

| | |
|---|---|
| **Claudio:** | Thus answer I in the name of Benedick, |
| | But hear these ill news with the ears of Claudio. |
| | 'Tis certain so, the prince woos for himself. |
| | Friendship is constant in all other things |
| | Save in the office and affairs of love. |
| | Therefore, all hearts in love use their own tongues, |
| | Let every eye negotiate for itself |
| | And trust no agent, for beauty is a witch |
| | Against whose charms faith melteth into blood. |
| | This is an accident of hourly proof, |
| | Which I mistrusted not. Farewell, therefore, Hero! |

(Act 2, Scene 1)

2) Read Act 3, Scene 1 from "**Why, you speak truth.**" to "**How much an ill word may empoison liking.**" Then answer the questions below.

   a) How is Hero presented in this extract?

   b) Write about the importance of criticism in the play. You should consider:
   - times when characters criticise each other
   - how different characters respond to being criticised.

3) Read Act 3, Scene 3 from the beginning of the scene to "**thank God you are rid of a knave.**" How does Shakespeare use Dogberry and the Watch to create humour? You should refer to this extract and to the play as a whole.

## Honour and Reputation

Everyone in Messina is a massive gossip — pretty scary in a society where your honour is worth dying for...

### Honour is earned and defended

1) The **male** characters believe in a strict **moral code** influenced by **chivalry** and medieval **knights** — a man was considered **honourable** if he was **admired** by others for his **bravery**, **honesty** and **loyalty**.

2) Claudio has honour "<u>bestowed</u>" on him for his **bravery** in **battle**. The opinions of **highly-ranked** individuals like Don Pedro (a prince) were important in gaining **honour**.

3) **Duels** were used to resolve **conflict** and restore **honour** — it meant you were willing to **risk** your **life** to defend your **actions**. To **deny** a duel was **dishonourable** — Claudio has to accept Benedick's challenge or be a seen as a "<u>coward</u>".

4) Honour was **not** just a **personal** concern — a **family's** actions reflected on the **head** of the **household**.

A **woman's** honour depended on her being '**pure**'. When Hero is accused of being **dishonourable**, Leonato is also dishonoured and would rather **die** than live with the **shame**: "<u>hath no man's dagger here a point for me?</u>"

### Everyone is concerned with their reputation

1) **Reputation** is important at all levels of **society** in the play — the **lower-status** characters are concerned about their **reputation** just like the **nobles**. Dogberry is very **offended** when Conrade calls him "<u>an ass</u>".

2) Don John uses the characters' **fear** of **losing honour** and **reputation** to **manipulate** them. When he tells Claudio that Hero has been disloyal, he says "<u>it would better fit your honour to change your mind</u>" about marrying her.

3) The play explores the effects of **slander** (spreading **lies**). Hero recognises "<u>how much an ill word may empoison liking</u>" — this is demonstrated when the men slander her in Act 4.

4) Hero's **reputation** is temporarily **destroyed**. Without her **honour**, she is **nothing** — even Leonato calls her "<u>foul-tainted</u>". She pretends to be **dead** rather than **suffer** the effects of slander.

> **TARGET GRADE** (8-9)
>
> When Claudio describes Hero as "Done to death by slanderous tongues" in Act 5, Scene 3, Shakespeare is using a technique called 'synecdoche'. This is where a part of something is used to refer to the whole. Here, the tongues represent Messina's gossiping citizens, depersonalising them so that they seem remote and menacing.

### Elizabethans believed in a strict social hierarchy

1) The **Great Chain of Being** was a rigid system that claimed that the **social order** had been **established** by **God**. People were **born** with a certain **status** because God had decided it.

2) The noble characters are **aware** of everyone's **social status** and believe it is important to **maintain** the **social hierarchy**. Don John says it would be **wrong** for Don Pedro to **marry** Hero because "<u>she is no equal for his birth</u>" — marrying someone of **lower status** could **damage** his **reputation**.

> **Character — Don John**
>
> Don John was **born** outside of marriage and is illegitimate. He feels **isolated** from society — this gives him a motive for **disrupting** the **social order**.

**EXAM TIP**

### Show how different characters protect their reputation...

Honour has its upsides and its downsides. Claudio is praised for being an honourable man, but his need to protect his reputation allows him to be tricked by Don John and causes him to act badly towards Hero.

# Love and Marriage

In Shakespeare's time, marriage for high-status people was more like a business deal between a man and a woman's father. Very romantic. But if you were really lucky, someone might write you a soppy poem...

## Marriages were rarely about love

1) In Elizabethan society, **marriages** were often **arranged** to bring **financial** or **social** benefit to both families.

2) Claudio claims that he **loves** Hero, but that **isn't** the **only reason** he wants to marry her:

| Hero is pure | Hero is a noblewoman | Hero is rich |
|---|---|---|
| Claudio describes Hero as <u>"a modest young lady"</u> — it is important that his wife has a good **reputation**. | Claudio is a **count** and is friends with **high-status** people — his wife needs to match his **social status**. | Hero is Leonato's <u>"only heir"</u> — this means she will **inherit** all his **money** when he dies. |

3) In Act 5, Scene 1, Claudio agrees to **marry** someone he's never met to **earn** Leonato's **forgiveness**. He decides to <u>"embrace"</u> Leonato's offer — his **honour** is more important to him than his **feelings**.

4) **Women** usually had **little say** in their husbands — they had to **accept** their **father's** choice.

## Choosing a suitable partner was a serious business

© Alastair Muir / REX / Shutterstock

1) People were **expected** to get **married** — the characters are very **concerned** with finding **partners** for themselves and others.

2) Leonato **warns** Beatrice <u>"**thou wilt never get thee a husband**"</u> unless she **changes** her behaviour. She and Benedick **ignore** society's **expectations** about what makes a 'suitable' partner.

3) Claudio feels that <u>"**time goes on crutches**"</u> until he can marry Hero — once he has found someone **worthy** to be his wife, he is **eager** to get married **straightaway**.

## The characters enjoy playing Cupid

1) Both of the **romances** in the play happen because of **intervention** from the other characters. Don Pedro **woos** Hero for Claudio and suggests the **plan** to **unite** Benedick and Beatrice.

2) The characters use **classical imagery** to describe their **matchmaking** — this makes the plans sound **dramatic** and **heroic**. They see themselves as **playing** the **role** of "**love-gods**" and Hero says that **tricking** Beatrice will be like shooting "<u>**Cupid's crafty arrow**</u>".

> **Character — Don Pedro**
>
> Don Pedro **supports** his **friends** by trying to find **suitable** partners for them. He sees **matchmaking** as an enjoyable **challenge**, saying they will have Cupid's "<u>glory</u>" when the plans succeed.

3) Shakespeare creates **comedy** in the **tricks** that bring Benedick and Beatrice together. The **dramatic irony** creates **humour** for the **audience** — they know about Don Pedro's **plan** so it is amusing to watch Benedick and Beatrice **fall for** the **tricks**.

4) However, the tricks raise **questions** about how **real** their relationship is. Benedick and Beatrice seem **made for** each other, but their relationship is the result of **deception**. The audience might **question** whether they would have ended up **together** if they hadn't been **tricked** into it.

# Love and Marriage

## Noble men followed the courtly love tradition

1) A courtly lover was **expected** to write **poems** or **songs** to **praise** and **impress** the woman he loved. He would also send her **gifts**, such as the **perfumed gloves** Hero receives from Claudio.

2) Claudio and Hero **represent** this **traditional** type of love. They often speak in **verse** and Claudio dramatically **praises** Hero. He uses the **metaphor** of a "<u>jewel</u>" and the **superlative** "<u>the sweetest lady</u>" to describe her.

See p.52 for more on imagery.

3) Shakespeare **criticises** the courtly love tradition — he presents it as **shallow** and **less meaningful** than a relationship like Benedick and Beatrice's, which is based on **real love**.

## Benedick and Beatrice reject courtly love traditions

1) Benedick and Beatrice don't have a **traditional** courtship — instead of wooing, they **insult** each other **wittily**, usually in **prose**.

2) Shakespeare uses them to **mock** the **courtly love** tradition. When they do fall in love, their **love** seems more **real** than Claudio and Hero's.

© Sam Goldwyn / Renaissance / BBC / Kobal / REX / Shutterstock

3) From the start of the play, Shakespeare shows that Benedick is **not** like **courtly lovers**. In Act 1, Scene 1, he isn't **impressed** by Hero's **beauty** and refuses to "<u>praise</u>" her as Claudio expects him to.

4) Beatrice **criticises** the courtly love tradition as **unmanly** — "<u>manhood is melted into curtsies</u>". She expects **more** from a man and wants Benedick to **prove** his love for her by **killing** Claudio.

5) However, Beatrice and Benedick **follow** some **traditions** of courtly love. In Act 5, Scene 4, it's revealed that they've written **poems** to each other. Benedick also **shaves** and wears **perfume** to impress Beatrice.

6) They **aren't** completely **opposed** to love — they just want to have a relationship on their **own terms**.

## Love makes characters act differently

1) When the characters fall in love, their personalities **change**. For example, Claudio **replaces** his "<u>war-thoughts</u>" with "<u>soft and delicate desires</u>".

2) In Act 2, Scene 3, Benedick describes someone who falls in love as "<u>a fool</u>". It is **comic** when he **changes** his mind later in the scene and decides to be "<u>horribly in love</u>".

3) After the tricks, Benedick is quieter and says he has "<u>toothache</u>", while Beatrice is moody and says she is "<u>sick</u>". This **lovesick** behaviour is very **different** from their usual **confidence** and **quick wit**.

4) Shakespeare presents their **lovesick** behaviour for **comic effect** and to **mock** traditional lovers.

> **Shakespeare's Techniques — Imagery**
>
> Shakespeare uses **imagery** related to **music** to suggest **love** makes **men** more **gentle**. Claudio swaps **military** music ("<u>the drum and fife</u>") for courtly music (the "<u>tabor and the pipe</u>") and Benedick's **spirit** "<u>is crept into a lute-string</u>".

---

**KEY QUOTE**

### "I do love nothing in the world so well as you"

Benedick and Beatrice often struggle to discuss their love in public, but in private they're open about their feelings. Claudio talks about his love for Hero to anyone who'll listen — well, except for Hero herself...

# Deception and Misunderstanding

Deception is a huge theme in this play. There's a funny side to it, but it causes a whole lot of problems too.

## Deception and misunderstanding have comic effects...

1) A lot of the play's **humour** is created when characters are **deceived** or **misunderstand** situations. The **audience** knows the **truth** about what's happening and **enjoys** waiting for the characters to **catch up**.

2) Some characters **intentionally** deceive other characters, such as in the **tricks** to make Benedick and Beatrice fall in love. Others **misunderstand** things, such as when Antonio tells Leonato that **Don Pedro** wants to marry Hero.

3) Dogberry's **confusion** with **words** provides **comedy** to distract from the romances. He tries to use **sophisticated language** without knowing what the words **mean**. When Leonato calls him "<u>tedious</u>", he **misunderstands** and thinks that it's a **compliment**.

> **Shakespeare's Techniques — Setting**
>
> Antonio's servant overhears Don Pedro in a "<u>thick-pleached alley</u>" (a walkway covered by **branches**). When Beatrice is tricked, she overhears Hero and Ursula in a "<u>pleached bower</u>" (a shelter covered by **branches**). These places allow characters to **listen** without being **seen**, making them an excellent **setting** for **deception**.

## ... but they also threaten the happy ending of the play

1) Don John causes **problems** for the characters when he **deceives** Don Pedro and Claudio.

> **Shakespeare's Techniques — Antithesis**
>
> Shakespeare sets up Don Pedro and Don John as **opposites**. Don Pedro uses **deception** to achieve Cupid's "<u>glory</u>", but Don John uses deception to **destroy** happiness and to "<u>build mischief</u>".

2) They quickly **believe** Don John's '**evidence**' that Hero has been **unfaithful** — even though Don John is **not** a **trustworthy** character.

3) Their **mistrust** of **women** means that they find it **easy** to believe that the **accusations** are true.

4) Don John's deception nearly **destroys** Claudio and Hero's **relationship** — he **refuses** to **marry** her.

5) Hero's **reputation** is almost **ruined** — she'd have been sent to a **nunnery** if the truth hadn't come out.

6) Beatrice wants Claudio **dead** and Benedick challenges him to a **duel**. These **obstacles** are only **overcome** when Don John's **plot** is **exposed** and the characters realise they have been **deceived**.

## Deception ultimately unites the couples

1) The deceptions of Beatrice and Benedick are **light-hearted** and **playful**. The two scenes **mirror** each other, which shows how **similar** the characters are.

2) The tricking encourages them to **reflect** on their **behaviour** and become **better** people. Benedick **changes** his mind about **marriage**, admitting "<u>I must not seem proud</u>" and Beatrice exclaims "<u>Contempt, farewell, and maiden pride, adieu!</u>"

3) The successful deceptions mark a **turning point** in the comedy and an important **change** in their relationship.

© Alastair Muir / REX / Shutterstock

4) Deception is also used to **restore** Hero's **reputation** and bring her and Claudio back **together**. Hero **pretends** to be **dead**, then she comes to the wedding in **disguise** so that Claudio can marry her 'cousin'. The **damage** caused by Don John's **deception** is **erased**.

# Deception and Misunderstanding

## The characters are usually watching each other

1) There are lots of references to 'noting' (noticing) in the play:

- Claudio **notes** Hero in Act 1, Scene 1 and asks Benedick "<u>didst thou note the daughter of Signior Leonato?</u>" Benedick says "<u>I noted her not, but I looked on her</u>", which shows that **different people** note **different things**.

- Don Pedro says Benedick will be a "<u>notable argument</u>" (something worth talking about) if he ever falls in **love**. The male characters **look for** opportunities to **mock** each other.

- Balthasar makes a **pun** about **musical notes** and noting — "<u>There's not a note of mine that's worth the noting.</u>" He suggests that they shouldn't pay **attention** to anything in the song — just as the characters shouldn't pay attention to any of the **gossip** they hear, because none of it is **true**.

> There's even a reference to noting the play's title, as 'Nothing' would have been pronounced as 'noting' — see p.2.

### Shakespeare's Techniques — Song

Before the men **trick** Benedick, Balthasar sings a **song** that references the **deception** and "<u>fraud of men</u>" in the play. He sings "<u>Men were deceivers ever</u>" and "<u>constant never</u>" in their **love**. Shakespeare highlights the **untrustworthy** nature of **men**, which **hints** at the deception and tricks to come.

2) Most of the characters are staying at **Leonato's house** — this **claustrophobic setting** gives them lots of opportunities to **observe** each other, which can lead to them being **deceived**:

- Benedick and Beatrice **observe** and **overhear** their friends in the orchard and are **tricked** into falling in love.

- Claudio and Don Pedro **observe** Borachio with Margaret and are **tricked** into believing she is Hero.

## Outward appearances can hide the truth

1) The characters **observe** each other, but worry about whether things are really as they 'seem'.

2) Claudio believes "<u>beauty is a witch</u>" — he knows **appearances** can be **deceptive**. When he hears Don John's lies about Hero, he believes that he's been **deceived** by her **beauty** — he thinks her **innocent** appearance has **hidden** her "<u>savage sensuality</u>".

### Shakespeare's Techniques — Imagery

Claudio uses the **metaphor** of a "<u>rotten orange</u>" to describe how he thinks Hero is **different** from how she **appeared** — she is **beautiful** on the **outside** but on the **inside** she is **decaying** and **damaged**.

3) Beatrice and Benedick give the **impression** they have a "<u>merry war</u>", but they are tricked into **showing** their **hidden** desires. When they finally **admit** their **love**, their **happy ending** is **satisfying** for the audience.

4) The theme of **false appearances** is highlighted by the **masked ball**. It shows the love of **disguise** and **deception** in Messina — the characters enjoy pretending to be other people and deceiving each other.

5) When Hero is **revealed** as **alive** in the final scene, this ends the **misunderstandings** and **disguise** in the play.

© Sam Golovan / Renaissance / BBC / Kobal EX / Shutterstock

### KEY QUOTE

## "I cannot hide what I am"

Ironically, Don John claims that he won't pretend to be something he's not — he can't hide his feelings and openly admits to being a villain. But he has no trouble lying and playing tricks when it suits him.

# Gender

The play's female characters get a rubbish deal — it was a tough life for women back in Shakespeare's day.

## Women had little power in Elizabethan society

> A patriarchal society is one where men have authority and dominance over women.

1) The Elizabethans lived in a **patriarchal** society — life was **controlled** by **men**. Like Hero, women were expected to be "<u>ruled</u>" by their **fathers** and **husbands**.

2) There were **few careers** available for noble women and they often had **no way** to live **independently**. As **unmarried** women, Hero and Beatrice live in Leonato's house with him as their **guardian**.

3) The **father** was the **head** of the household and the **mother** had **little power**. **Childbirth** was **dangerous** and many women **died** giving birth — this might explain why the **mothers** are **missing** from the play.

In the play, the men have all the **power**, and Shakespeare shows that they often don't use it **wisely** — they make **mistakes** and they **judge** women **harshly**. In contrast, the female characters are often **powerless** to help themselves, but have **good** intentions and are **loyal** to each other.

**TARGET GRADE** 8-9

Benedick's love for Beatrice gives her some power to influence the events of the play. To prove his love, Benedick offers to do "anything" for her. This allows Beatrice to access some of his power as a man. She asks him to kill Claudio, using her limited power to defend Hero's honour — this shows her loyalty to Hero and willingness to exploit Benedick's love to defend her.

## Women had strict expectations to follow...

1) Noble women only received a **narrow education** that mainly focused on **household affairs** — their role was to get **married** and provide **children** to continue the **family line**. This kept **property** and **wealth** within the family.

2) Women were expected to be '**pure**' and remain **virgins** until **marriage**. Claudio's **accusations** that Hero "**knows the heat of a luxurious bed**" would've been very **serious** — no **respectable** man would marry her.

3) Leonato is **devastated** by the accusations — if Hero **can't** make a good **marriage**, he thinks her life is **over**.

**Character — Friar Francis**

The Friar believes it'd be better for an '**impure**' woman with a "<u>wounded reputation</u>" to live **away** from **society**. He advises Leonato to **hide** Hero "<u>in some reclusive and religious life</u>" (a **nunnery**).

## ... but not all women conformed to them

1) The most **important** figure in Elizabethan society was a **woman** who **defied** expectations of **female** behaviour. **Queen Elizabeth I** was a **strong ruler** who **never married** and didn't have **children** — this **challenged** traditional attitudes towards **women** at the time.

Photo by Reg Wilson © RSC.

2) Shakespeare was **influenced** by these **changing attitudes** to women when creating **strong-willed, independent** female characters like **Beatrice**.

3) Beatrice **answers back** to men — she knows her **wit** and **intelligence** are a **match** for theirs.

4) However, she does **conform** to **marriage**, and Benedick **stops** her talking with a **kiss** — "<u>I will stop your mouth.</u>" Despite their **unconventional** relationship, this could be seen as a sign of his new **power** and **authority** over her.

---

EXAM TIP

## Discuss how characters respond to gender expectations...

Beatrice is a woman ahead of her time. In contrast, Hero's passive behaviour might seem strange to a modern audience, but she's a product of her society and behaves as she would have been expected to.

# Loyalty

Personally, I think it's weird to trust a bloke who you know really, really doesn't like you and who you've just fought a war against. But clearly that's just me, as the men believe any old story that Don John tells them...

## The men are good friends...

1) At the **beginning** of the play, Don Pedro, Claudio and Benedick are good **friends**. They have **fought** together in **battle** and have developed **close bonds**.

2) Don Pedro **proves** his **loyalty** to Claudio. He woos Hero to "<u>obtain her</u>" for Claudio and **promises** to "<u>join with thee to disgrace her</u>".

> **Context**
>
> In Elizabethan times, many men feared that their **wives** would be **disloyal** and they would be 'cuckolded' (see p.53). Don John **plays** on this **fear** to encourage the **shaming** of Hero, and Benedick **refuses** to **marry** since he will "<u>trust none</u>".

## ... but they don't always trust each other

1) Claudio is **quick** to believe Don John's **lie** that Don Pedro is **wooing** Hero for himself — he says "<u>Friendship is constant in all other things / Save in the office and affairs of love</u>".

2) Claudio sees Don Pedro as a **rival** — he doesn't **trust** that Don Pedro will be **loyal** to him when it comes to **love**.

3) Benedick is **less loyal** to the **men** in the play — Beatrice claims that "<u>He hath every month a new sworn brother</u>", suggesting he is **not committed** to his **friendships**.

4) When Benedick's loyalty is **tested**, he **chooses** Beatrice over Claudio and even **challenges** Claudio to a duel. This suggests his **relationship** with Beatrice is more **important** to him than his **friendships**.

Photo by Reg Wilson © RSC.

## Family loyalties are complicated

1) Beatrice is fiercely **loyal** to Hero — she believes on her "<u>soul</u>" that Hero is **innocent** and insists "<u>as sure as I have a thought</u>" that Claudio is **wrong**. In Act 4, Scene 1, she shows that she would put her **loyalty** to Hero **above** her **love** for Benedick — she tells him "<u>Farewell</u>" when he **refuses** to **duel** Claudio.

2) Leonato needs **convincing** of Hero's innocence before he **defends** her — at first he **believes** the **men** over his daughter and says "<u>These hands shall tear her</u>" if she is **guilty**.

> **Character — Antonio**
>
> Antonio shows **loyalty** to his **brother** by supporting him when he **challenges** Claudio to a duel. He calls Claudio and Don Pedro "<u>boys, apes, braggarts, Jacks, milksops!</u>" The list of **insults** shows how **passionately** he supports Leonato.

3) Once he is convinced she is **innocent**, Leonato fiercely **defends** Hero. He **challenges** Claudio to a "<u>trial of a man</u>", which shows he would **die** to clear her **name**.

4) Don John is **disloyal** to his brother — he has recently **fought** against him. Don Pedro has tried to **repair** their relationship, but Don John is only interested in **revenge**. He **manipulates** his brother into believing Hero is **impure**.

---

**KEY QUOTE**

## "O, on my soul, my cousin is belied!"

Beatrice's first loyalty is to Hero — she defends her from the moment she is accused. The male characters are often suspicious of each other and their loyalties change quickly, but Beatrice always has Hero's back.

# Practice Questions

Have a go at the questions below to see if you know the play's themes inside out...

## Quick Questions

1) Why does Hero's honour affect Leonato?

2) What was the purpose of duels in Shakespeare's time?

3) Give two reasons why Claudio thinks Hero would be a suitable wife for him.

4) Give two examples of what a courtly lover was expected to do.

5) Explain how deception brings about the play's happy ending.

6) Give an example of 'noting' in the play.

7) Why does Claudio describe Hero as a "rotten orange"?

8) What did Elizabethan society believe a woman's role was?

For even more practice, try the Much Ado About Nothing Sudden Fail Quiz — just scan this QR code!

**Sudden Fail Quiz**

## In-depth Questions

1) Who do you think is the most honourable character in the play? Explain your answer.

2) Do you think that Benedick and Beatrice would have ended up together without Don Pedro's plan? Why / why not?

3) Overall, do you think Shakespeare presents deception as harmless or dangerous? Explain your answer.

4) Do you think that Beatrice wants to be more like a conventional Elizabethan woman? Use examples from the play to explain your answer.

5) Explain how Benedick's and Don Pedro's loyalties are different in the play.

## Target Grade 8-9

1) Explore how Margaret's lower social status might affect her actions in the play. You should consider her reputation in your answer.

# Practice Questions

Now you know all about the themes, here's a chance to put that knowledge into action — get stuck into these exciting exam-style questions. Take five minutes to plan your answer — it'll help you explain your ideas clearly.

## Exam-style Questions

1) Write about how ideas about love are presented in the play.
   Refer to the extract from Act 1, Scene 1 below and to the play as a whole.

   | | |
   |---|---|
   | **Claudio:** | My liege, your highness now may do me good. |
   | **Don Pedro:** | My love is thine to teach. Teach it but how, And thou shalt see how apt it is to learn Any hard lesson that may do thee good. |
   | **Claudio:** | Hath Leonato any son, my lord? |
   | **Don Pedro:** | No child but Hero, she's his only heir. Dost thou affect her, Claudio? |
   | **Claudio:** | O, my lord, When you went onward on this ended action, I looked upon her with a soldier's eye, That liked, but had a rougher task in hand Than to drive liking to the name of love; But now I am returned and that war-thoughts Have left their places vacant, in their rooms Come thronging soft and delicate desires, All prompting me how fair young Hero is, Saying, I liked her ere I went to wars. |
   | **Don Pedro:** | Thou wilt be like a lover presently And tire the hearer with a book of words. If thou dost love fair Hero, cherish it, And I will break with her and with her father, And thou shalt have her. Was't not to this end That thou began'st to twist so fine a story? |

   (Act 1, Scene 1)

2) Read Act 2, Scene 1 from "**By my troth, niece**" to "**as merry as the day is long.**"
   How does Shakespeare present the characters' expectations of women in this extract
   and in the rest of the play?

3) Read Act 3, Scene 3 from "**Not so, neither.**" to "**You'll be made bring Deformed forth**".
   Explore the importance of misunderstandings in this extract and in the rest of the play.

4) Read Act 5, Scene 1 from "**But when shall we set the savage bull's horns**" to
   "**Did he not say my brother was fled?**", then answer the questions below.

   a) How is Benedick presented in this extract?

   b) In this extract, Benedick has chosen loyalty to Beatrice over loyalty to his friends.
      Write about the significance of loyalty in the play.

# Form and Structure of 'Much Ado About Nothing'

Form and structure have a big impact on a play — writers have to make sure that everything fits together properly, the plot makes sense and the audience isn't going to nod off. Shakespeare does a great job of this.

## 'Much Ado About Nothing' is a comedy...

1) Shakespeare wrote three **different types** of play — **tragedy**, **comedy** and **history**. *Much Ado About Nothing* contains lots of the **features** commonly used in his **comedies**, including:

- A happy ending
- Disguises
- Music and dancing
- Young lovers
- Marriage
- Puns and wordplay

2) In a **comedy**, there's normally a **problem** at the beginning of the play that is **solved** by the end of it — the audience is **confident** that everything will **end well** for the main characters.

3) In *Much Ado About Nothing*, there **isn't** a large problem right away — it only develops **later** in the play when Don John plans to **disrupt** the wedding.

4) Shakespeare's comedies also usually feature some **lower-status** characters who are included to make the audience **laugh**. Dogberry and Verges distract the audience from the main plots — their **misunderstandings** and **incompetence** create **humour**.

© Nigel Norrington / ArenaPAL

### Shakespeare's Techniques — Foreshadowing

The **title** of the play **foreshadows** its **happy ending**. It says that the characters make a lot of **fuss** ("Ado") about "**Nothing**", which suggests that everything will be **fine** in the **end**.

## ... but there are serious parts too

1) The play sometimes seems **tragic**, such as when Hero is accused at the wedding in Act 4, Scene 1. If the Watch hadn't **discovered** the **plot**, Hero might **not** have been proved **innocent** and the play might **not** have ended **happily**.

2) Don John will "**endeavour any thing**" to cause **trouble**, and his plots **threaten** the **happy ending**.

3) The characters **learn** and **change** by the end of the play. The **challenges** that the characters face make the play more **exciting** and mean that the **happy ending** is more **satisfying** for the audience.

### Claudio

Claudio has to **earn forgiveness** and make up for his treatment of Hero. As a traditional **romantic hero**, he has to face **challenges** to become **worthy** of marrying the woman he loves.

### Benedick and Beatrice

Beatrice and Benedick each have to **overcome** their **pride**. They admit that they have **flaws** and want to become **better** people. They show **vulnerability** and admit their true **feelings** for each other.

4) Despite the **happy ending**, there is **no guarantee** that the couples will be **happy** together in the **future**.

See p.53 for more about cuckolds.

5) Benedick and Claudio are still making **jokes** about **marriage** and **cuckolds** at the end of the play — their attitudes haven't **changed** completely. This suggests that they still think the **women** could be **unfaithful**.

# Form and Structure of 'Much Ado About Nothing'

## The play has a five act structure

Acts 1, 2 and 3 lead to the **climax** in Act 4 and everything is **resolved** in Act 5:

- Act 1 **introduces** the main characters and **sets up** Don John as a **threat** to the comedy.
- Act 2 **develops** the **romances** between Beatrice & Benedick and Claudio & Hero.
- Act 3 **threatens** the **happy ending** as Claudio is **tricked** by Don John.
- Act 4 presents the most significant **obstacle** to be overcome as Hero is **accused** at the wedding.
- Act 5 is the **resolution** — the **truth** is revealed and there is a **happy ending** for both couples.

## Shakespeare weaves the two romance plots together

1) The two relationships **mirror** each other throughout the play.

2) This structure means the **traditional** courtship of Claudio and Hero can be directly **compared** with the **unconventional** relationship of Beatrice and Benedick, who are "**too wise to woo peaceably.**"

3) Shakespeare uses **antithesis** and presents the **couples** as **opposites** — when things are going **well** for one couple, they are often going **badly** for the other couple:

*See p.54 for more on antithesis.*

| Acts 1-2 | Claudio **loves** Hero... | ... but Beatrice and Benedick **insult** each other. |
|---|---|---|
| Act 3 | Claudio believes **lies** about Hero... | ... but Benedick and Beatrice are **falling in love**. |
| Act 4 | Claudio **accuses** Hero... | ... but Beatrice and Benedick declare their **love**. |

4) The two romance plots **come together** in Act 5 and both end in **marriage**. This fulfils the audience's **expectations** of how a **comedy** should end — all the **obstacles** have been **overcome**.

## The acts take place over different amounts of time

1) Claudio's engagement to Hero happens very **quickly** — it's the **same day** that the men **arrive** in Messina. He wants to get married **straightaway**, but Leonato tells him they must **wait** "**a just seven-night**" (a week).

2) This week creates **time** in the play for the rest of Act 2 and then Act 3 to happen — the **pace** is **relaxed** and the characters **enjoy** tricking Benedick and Beatrice.

3) However, it also allows time for Don John's **scheming**. The audience has to **wait** from Act 2, Scene 2 until Act 4, Scene 1 to see whether his plan to ruin the wedding **succeeds** — this creates **dramatic tension**.

4) Acts 4 and 5 take place in much **less time** — this **increases** the **pace** towards the **end** of the play. Once the **truth** comes out, everything is **resolved** quickly.

## Explain how the play's structure helps create tension...

Even in a comedy, you can't have joke after joke after joke — it would get less funny after a while. Shakespeare creates highs and lows in the plot to make things varied and keep the audience interested.

# Dramatic Irony

The characters have no idea what's going on half the time, but the audience gets to be a right know-it-all.

## Dramatic irony is a key dramatic device in the play

1) Dramatic irony is when the **audience** is **aware** of something that **characters don't know** about yet. There are **two** main ways that this happens:

### Events on stage

The audience **sees** events **on stage** that other characters don't **know** about. For example, they see the Watch arrest Borachio, but most **characters** only **find out** about this **later**.

### Soliloquies

Sometimes characters reveal their **thoughts** in a **soliloquy** (see p.51), such as when Beatrice speaks about her changing feelings in Act 3, Scene 1. She is **alone** on stage — only the audience knows when she says she will tame her "<u>wild heart</u>" for Benedick.

2) Dramatic irony **emphasises** the theme of 'noting' — the audience **observes** the characters just as they **observe** each other. In the play, characters **note** things that are intended to **deceive** them and they **believe** what they see. Dramatic irony means that the audience **aren't deceived** — they always know the **truth**.

## It creates humour...

Shakespeare uses dramatic irony for **comic** effect, such as when Benedick is tricked into falling in love:

- At the **start** of Act 2, Scene 3, Benedick says that he will **never** be "<u>such a fool</u>" as to fall in **love**.

- It's **humorous** when he says this — the audience **knows** about Don Pedro's **plan** to make him fall in love, so they **expect** that he will soon **change his mind**.

- It's also **comic** when he does fall in **love** — by the **end** of the scene, Benedick says Beatrice's love for him "<u>must be requited</u>" (returned).

## ... but it also creates dramatic tension

1) The **audience** knows that Don John has **deceived** Claudio and that Hero is **innocent**, but they **can't** do anything about it.

2) Act 3, Scene 5 is **tense** for the audience — they **know** that Dogberry has information that could **stop** Claudio shaming Hero. Leonato **doesn't know** this — it's **frustrating** when he tells them he is in "<u>great haste</u>" and leaves.

3) There is also **tension** when Benedick **challenges** Claudio. He is **serious** at this point, **contrasting** with his **comic** behaviour elsewhere. He has agreed to **duel** Claudio for Beatrice and the audience doesn't know whether Don John's **plot** will be **revealed** before this happens.

### Shakespeare's Techniques — Form

The **form** of the play also creates dramatic irony. Despite the moments of **tension**, the play is a **comedy**, so the audience expects it to **end happily**. The characters **don't know** if they will **overcome** their **problems**, but the audience **knows** that everything will be **resolved** in the end.

## Write about the effect of dramatic irony on the audience...

Dramatic irony makes the audience feel more involved in the play. It's almost like they're a participant in the tricks — they know what the plan is and who's being deceived, but the characters don't have a clue.

# Mood and Atmosphere

It's important to get the right mood in a scene — it's no good if the audience starts laughing at the sad parts...

## The mood is mostly playful...

1) The play is full of **humorous tricks** and **witty conversations** — these help to create a **light-hearted** and **playful** mood.

2) The **setting** supports this atmosphere because it allows the characters to **relax**. Most of the scenes take place in Leonato's **house** and **garden** — the characters are **separated** from the issues of the **outside world**.

3) This **domestic** and **peaceful** setting of Messina **contrasts** with the **battlefields** the men have returned from.

4) Claudio declares that "war-thoughts" have left his mind and instead the soldiers are able to **enjoy** themselves. The **masked ball** and **matchmaking** create a **cheerful** and **lively** atmosphere.

5) **Comic characters** like Dogberry and the Watch provide **humour** — they are used to **lighten** the **mood**.

**Shakespeare's Techniques — Symbolism**

The garden provides the perfect **setting** for **playful trickery**. It also **symbolises** youth and fertility — this makes it the ideal setting for Beatrice and Benedick to fall in **love**. Shakespeare is suggesting their love is **natural** and **genuine**.

## ... but it can also be tense and tragic

1) **Tension** is created by the **serious** events in the play, like Don John's **scheming** and the **shaming** of Hero.

© Sam Goldwyn / Renaissance / BBC / Kobal / REX / Shutterstock

2) When Hero is accused at the wedding, the **language** is very **harsh** — Claudio calls her "an approved wanton" (a sexually promiscuous woman) and Leonato says "Let her die." The audience feels **uncomfortable** about Hero's treatment and **frustrated** that Claudio has fallen for Don John's **lies**.

3) When Claudio and Don Pedro **mourn** at Hero's tomb, the **stage directions** say that some of the actors are carrying "tapers" — this shows that the stage is lit by **torches**, which creates a **sombre** atmosphere.

## Music affects the mood of a scene

1) **Music** and **songs** provide **variety** from the spoken action and also help to create **different moods**.

2) At the **masked ball** and in the **final scene** of the play, music creates a **celebratory**, **joyful** mood and reflects the **carefree** atmosphere. The music accompanies the characters' dancing, which makes these scenes more **romantic**.

3) The "solemn hymn" at Hero's 'tomb' adds to the **sombre** atmosphere. This highlights Claudio's **grief** and concludes the **tragic** elements of the play before the **happy** final scene.

**Context**

Music is a **common** feature of Shakespeare's **comedies**. The main characters rarely sing — it's normally a **comic** or **minor** character. In this play, **Balthasar** doesn't have a **role** in the plot — he's just there to perform the songs.

KEY QUOTE

### "You have among you killed a sweet and innocent lady."

Don Pedro and Claudio don't realise Benedick's being serious when he challenges Claudio to a duel. The contrast between their jokes and Benedick's anger makes it tense and uncomfortable for the audience.

# Poetry and Prose

The bad news — poetry in Shakespeare can be a bit tricky and technical. The good news — this play doesn't have that much poetry in it. You still need to understand it though, so have a good read of these pages...

## Characters mostly speak in prose...

1) **Prose** is like **normal speech** — it **doesn't** usually have a fixed **rhythm**.

2) *Much Ado About Nothing* is mostly written in **prose**. This makes it **unusual** for a Shakespeare play — his plays **normally** contain much more **verse**.

3) This means that it's **significant** when characters **do** speak in **verse** in this play — verse is used at particularly **important** and **dramatic** moments. For example, the Friar speaks in verse when he describes his plan to "<u>Change slander to remorse</u>" by faking Hero's death.

© Sam Goldwyn / Renaissance / BBC / Kobal / REX/ Shutterstock

4) In Shakespeare's other plays, **lower-status** or **uneducated** characters would normally speak in **prose**, while **noble** characters would speak in **verse**.

5) This play is **unusual** because its **noble** characters often speak in **prose**. This works well with the **fast pace** of their dialogue and their **witty** conversations.

## ... but sometimes they speak in blank verse

1) **Blank verse** is a type of poetry that is carefully **measured** and **rhythmic**. It follows these **three rules**:

   - The lines usually **don't rhyme**.
   - Each line has **10 or 11** syllables.
   - Each line has a **5-beat** rhythm.

   | 1 | 2 | 3 | 4 | 5 |
   |---|---|---|---|---|

   Therefore, all **hearts** in **love** use **their** own **tongues**

2) Poetry with a 5-beat rhythm is called **iambic pentameter**. Each beat usually has one **stressed** and one **unstressed** syllable.

   *Iambic pentameter can be rhymed or unrhymed. Blank verse never rhymes.*

3) The **first syllable** in each **beat** is sounded **softly** — this is an **unstressed** syllable.

4) The **second syllable** in each **beat** is **emphasised** — this is a **stressed** syllable.

5) The **stressed** syllables **highlight** the most **significant** words in the line — "<u>hearts</u>", "<u>love</u>" and "<u>tongues</u>".

## Rhyming verse is used to make a point

1) Sometimes the poetry in the play **rhymes**. A **pair** of rhyming lines is called a **rhyming couplet**.

2) Hero uses a **rhyming couplet** after **tricking** Beatrice: This use of **rhyme** emphasises the **completion** of the **trick** and suggests that it has been **successful**.

   "If it prove so, then loving goes by **haps**; Some Cupid kills with arrows, some with **traps**." Act 3, Scene 1

3) Beatrice mostly speaks in **prose**, but uses **rhyming verse** when reflecting on her **feelings** for Benedick at the end of Act 3, Scene 1. This speech **marks** a **turning point** in their relationship and the use of **rhyme** reflects her **changing attitude** to love and to Benedick.

4) The Friar speaks in **rhyming verse** as Leonato and Hero leave after the wedding. This emphasises the **importance** of his **plan**, which is the "<u>cure</u>" that leads the play towards its **happy ending**.

# Poetry and Prose

## Claudio and Hero mostly speak in verse...

1) Claudio speaks in **blank verse** when he **accuses** Hero at the wedding. Hero does the same when she **reveals** she is **alive** at the end of the play. This **links** the scenes when the couple are **divided** and **reunited**.

2) Hero and Claudio's use of **blank verse** also reflects their **formal** and **traditional** approach to love. **Verse** and **poetry** are traditionally associated with **courtly love**.

3) Like a traditional **courtly lover**, Claudio uses **poetic** language full of **imagery** and **rhetoric** after he falls in **love** — Benedick says that Claudio's words have become a "<u>fantastical banquet</u>".

> **Character — Hero**
>
> Hero speaks **very little** in front of the **male** characters, but she speaks more **confidently** with the **female** characters. She **adapts** her speech to **conform** to society's **expectations**.

## ... but Benedick and Beatrice mostly speak in prose

1) Beatrice and Benedick speak **naturally** to each other in an **informal**, **familiar** way. This suggests they have a **close** and **genuine** connection.

2) They don't conduct their relationship in the way that **society** expects. Their use of **prose** highlights their **unconventional** attitudes and behaviour.

3) Benedick is **not** a typical **courtly lover** — he **rarely** speaks in **verse**. When he **struggles** to write a **poem** for Beatrice, he says "<u>I was not born under a rhyming planet</u>". Instead he expresses his **love** for Beatrice in his own way — in **witty prose**.

4) The noble characters use **prose** in **informal** situations. For example, Leonato speaks in **prose** with his **brother** Antonio, but uses **blank verse** in **public**, which reflects his **intelligence** and **status**.

5) Dogberry **only** speaks in **prose**. This suggests he isn't **intelligent** enough to **imitate** the verse used by the **noble** characters. When he tries to use **sophisticated** language like theirs, he gets the words **wrong**.

© Donald Cooper / photostage

**TARGET GRADE 8-9**

> Despite struggling with poetry, Benedick often speaks in an ornate style of prose called 'euphuism', which combines flowery language and techniques like alliteration, e.g. "One woman is fair, yet I am well; another is wise, yet I am well". Yet by Act 5, Scene 2, his speech has become less euphuistic — he says he must tell Beatrice "plainly" about his challenge to Claudio. This reflects how he has become more serious since falling in love with Beatrice.

## Soliloquies allow characters to speak honestly

1) A **soliloquy** is when a character speaks **alone** on **stage** — other characters **can't hear** what they're saying.

2) This technique means the **audience** can find out what a character is **thinking**, as they speak **openly**:

- Benedick and Beatrice each have a **soliloquy** after they are **tricked** — this shows the audience their **genuine** reactions to the tricks and allows them to **reveal** their **true feelings**.

- Claudio has a soliloquy when he thinks Don Pedro has **betrayed** him and wooed Hero for himself. This audience sees proof of Claudio's "<u>jealous complexion</u>" and how **easily** he can be **deceived**.

## Use technical terms like 'blank verse' in your answer...

The examiner wants you to show off what you've learnt, so try to use all the correct fancy terms when writing about Shakespeare's techniques. Just make sure you explain the effect of the techniques too.

# Imagery and Symbolism

Imagery makes the language more interesting, but it can sometimes make the play a bit tricky to understand.

## Clothing symbolises how quickly characters change

© Sam Goldwyn / Renaissance / BBC / Kobal / REX / Shutterstock

1) Shakespeare uses lots of references to **clothes** and **fashion**. This reflects how some characters are **fickle** in their feelings — they **change** their **emotions** as quickly as **fashions** change.

2) Claudio **changes** from admiring "<u>good armour</u>" to desiring "<u>the fashion of a new doublet</u>" (jacket). This change in taste **symbolises** his change from a **soldier** to a **lover** and his change in attitude towards **marriage**.

3) Antonio **insults** Don Pedro and Claudio by calling them "<u>fashion-monging boys</u>" ('fashion-crazy'). He's suggesting that they are more concerned with their **appearances** than with **genuine feelings**.

## Benedick and Beatrice are described with martial imagery

1) Shakespeare compares Benedick and Beatrice's **love** to a **battle** by describing it with **war-like** language.

2) At first, Beatrice and Benedick have a "<u>merry war</u>" — they **enjoy fighting** each other with **words**.

3) After Beatrice **insults** Benedick at the masked ball, Shakespeare uses **imagery** of **war** to show how much her words **hurt** him. He describes her words as "<u>poniards</u>" (a type of **dagger**) and uses **personification** to emphasise the **pain** they cause.

> *Personification is when human qualities are given to something non-human (like an object, an animal or an idea).*

"She speaks poniards and every word stabs."
Act 2, Scene 1

4) After the **tricks**, Claudio expects that Benedick and Beatrice will **stop fighting** — he says "<u>the two bears will not bite/ one another.</u>" This suggests their **hostile** relationship will become more **gentle** once they fall in **love**.

## Animal imagery shows that characters are caught by the tricks

1) **Hunting** imagery suggests that Don Pedro and the rest **enjoy** bringing Beatrice and Benedick together — phrases like "<u>pleasant'st angling</u>" and "<u>stalk on</u>" make it seem like a **sport** for the characters.

2) Hero uses a **simile** to compare Beatrice to a "<u>lapwing</u>" (a type of bird), which suggests she is moving **quickly** and **quietly**.

"For look where Beatrice like a lapwing runs"
Act 3, Scene 1

> *A simile is when one thing is described as being <u>like</u> something else.*

"see the fish Cut with her golden oars the silver stream, And greedily devour the treacherous bait"
Act 3, Scene 1

3) Ursula uses a **metaphor** about **fishing** to describe how Beatrice will **fall** for their **trick**.

> *A metaphor is when one thing is said to <u>be</u> something else.*

### "Taming my wild heart to thy loving hand"

Beatrice compares herself to a wild animal — she has always rejected society's expectations. Getting married means she'll have to be 'tamed' and conform to society, but she's willing to do that for Benedick.

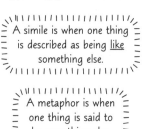

# Puns and Wordplay

The info on this page will really help your — wait for it — *pun*derstanding of language and wordplay. You might say it's a *pun*damental skill for the exam. Thankfully Shakespeare's a bit better at this than I am...

## Shakespeare uses language playfully

1) Shakespeare uses a lot of **puns** — **jokes** that play on the **different meanings** of a **word** or **similar words**.

2) Puns are often made when a character deliberately **twists** the **meaning** of a word.

3) Beatrice turns **praise** of Benedick into an **insult**. The messenger describes Benedick as "<u>**stuffed with all honourable virtues**</u>". Beatrice responds that Benedick is a "<u>**stuffed man**</u>", suggesting he is **lazy** and **fat**.

4) There are lots of **sexual** puns in the play. For example, when Claudio and Leonato claim that Beatrice has written **love poetry** for Benedick, they make a pun about the word "<u>**sheet**</u>".

> "when she had writ it, and was reading it over, she found 'Benedick' and 'Beatrice' between the sheet?"
>
> Act 2, Scene 3

5) This could refer to the **poem**, which was written on **paper** ("<u>the sheet</u>"), but it could also mean that Benedick and Beatrice were in **bed** together.

## The men make lots of jokes about cuckolds

1) In Elizabethan times, if a woman **cheated** on a man, he was seen as **weak** and he became a **cuckold**. A cuckold was often shown as having **horns** on his **forehead**.

2) **Jokes** about cuckolds **frame** the play — the men talk about it at the **start** and at the **end**. In Act 1, Scene 1, Benedick jokingly asks whether Leonato is **sure** that he is Hero's **father** — "<u>**were you in doubt, sir?**</u>"

3) By the end of the play, Benedick wants to **marry** Beatrice even though he **risks** becoming a cuckold — he jokes about a **horn-tipped** walking stick, describing it as "<u>**reverend**</u>" (impressive).

© Photograph by Alastair Muir

## Dogberry's language provides a different kind of comedy

1) Shakespeare uses **wordplay** to make Dogberry a **comic** character. Dogberry tries to be **clever** with **language**, but he is humorous because of his **mistakes**, not his **jokes**.

**Context**

Shakespeare's **audience** would have **expected** this kind of **comic character**. The part of Dogberry was written for **Will Kemp**, a **clown** who played lots of Shakespeare's **comic** roles and was **popular** with audiences.

2) He often uses the **wrong words** in his speech. He proudly says that the Watch have "<u>**comprehended**</u>" (understood) two prisoners, when he means '**apprehended**' (arrested).

3) He **misunderstands** what other characters say to him — when the Sexton asks who the "<u>**malefactors**</u>" are (meaning the **prisoners** Borachio and Conrade), Dogberry replies "<u>**that am I and my partner**</u>".

## "pluck off the bull's horns and set them in my forehead"

Benedick enjoys his war of words with Beatrice, but most of his puns and jokes are about how much he dislikes women. He's convinced that any man who is daft enough to marry will end up as a cuckold.

# Other Language Techniques

Nearly there — this is the last page of Shakespeare's techniques, but here are a few more just to finish off.

## Contrasts are important in this play

1) **Antithesis** is a literary device where two **contrasting** ideas are put **together**.

*Antithesis means 'opposite'.*

2) Claudio uses **antithesis** to describe Hero at the wedding. This shows the **contrast** between the **honourable** person he thought she was and the **unfaithful** woman he now believes her to be.

> "But fare thee well, **most foul**, **most fair**! Farewell, Thou **pure impiety** and **impious purity**!"
> Act 4, Scene 1

3) **Characters** are also presented as **opposites** to each other:

- Claudio is a traditional **courtly lover** and Benedick **rejects** courtly love.
- Hero is a **traditional** Elizabethan woman and Beatrice is more **unconventional**.
- Don Pedro tries to **bring** the couples **together** and Don John tries to **split** them up.

## Lists are used for dramatic effect

1) **Lists** can **emphasise** a point or **exaggerate** something.

2) Claudio lists the elements of Beatrice's **lovesick behaviour** to **convince** Benedick that she is in love with him — "<u>she falls, weeps, sobs, beats her heart, tears her hair, prays, curses</u>".

3) At the end of the masked ball, Benedick would rather do **anything** than **talk** to Beatrice. He **dramatically** lists all the things he would do in order to **avoid** her.

© Donald Cooper / photostage

4) Lists can also have a **comic** effect. In Act 5, Scene 1, Dogberry tries to **list** Borachio and Conrade's **crimes**, but ends up saying the **same** thing in six **different** ways.

## Repetition is used for comedy and emphasis

1) Dogberry's **confused** speech contains lots of **repetition**. He complains repeatedly that Conrade has called him "<u>an ass</u>", which **comically** emphasises how **outraged** he is.

2) Benedick uses **repetition** when giving his opinion of Hero — "<u>she's too low for a high praise, too brown for a fair praise and too little for a great praise.</u>" This emphasises how **judgmental** he is of **women**.

3) In Act 5, Scene 4, Benedick unknowingly references the trick his friends played on him — "<u>They swore that you were well-nigh dead for me.</u>" Beatrice says almost the same thing — "<u>They swore that you were almost sick for me.</u>" This repetition reflects how the tricking scenes **mirror** each other.

**TARGET GRADE** 8-9

When words are repeated at the beginning of multiple phrases, it is called 'anaphora'. 'Epistrophe' is when this happens at the <u>end</u> of phrases. Beatrice's dialogue uses epistrophe in Act 4, Scene 1 when she admits her love for Benedick: "believe me not; and yet I lie not." This makes her seem rambling and confused, which reflects how upset she is about the events of Hero's wedding.

## Write about the contrasts that appear in the play...

There are all sorts of pairs and parallels to spot in this play. Shakespeare creates these contrasts because he wants the audience to compare different characters, actions and ideas — so go on, get comparing...

# Practice Questions

Shakespeare's techniques might seem like a lot to get your head around, but they're important.

## Quick Questions

1) Give three common features of Shakespeare's comedies.

2) Describe an event from the play that uses dramatic irony.

3) Find two scenes where there is:   a) a playful mood     b) a tragic mood

4) "And got a calf in that same noble feat / Much like to you, for you have just his bleat."
Is this an example of...    a) blank verse     b) iambic pentameter?

5) Does Dogberry speak in prose or verse?

6) What does Shakespeare use animal imagery to describe?

7) "I found him here as melancholy as a lodge in a warren."
Is this...    a) a simile    b) a metaphor    c) personification?

8) What is a cuckold?

9) What is antithesis?

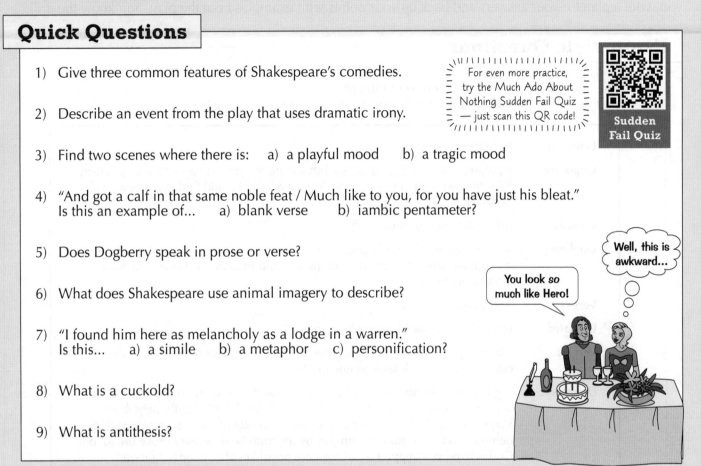

For even more practice, try the Much Ado About Nothing Sudden Fail Quiz — just scan this QR code!

Sudden Fail Quiz

You look *so* much like Hero!

Well, this is awkward...

## In-depth Questions

1) Why do you think Shakespeare uses lots of dramatic irony in the play?

2) Explain how Shakespeare uses wordplay to make Dogberry a comic character.

3) Describe a moment in the play that threatens the happy ending.
Explain the effect of this moment on the audience.

4) Why does Shakespeare give Benedick a soliloquy after he has been tricked in Act 2, Scene 3?

5) Find a pun in the play and explain what it means.

## Target Grade 8-9

1) Explain how Shakespeare uses antithesis to present Don Pedro and Don John.

2) Explore Shakespeare's use of repetition in Benedick and Beatrice's shared dialogue and
what this suggests about their relationship.  Give examples to support your answer.

# Practice Questions

Now you've swotted up on Shakespeare's techniques, it's time to tackle some exam-style questions. Make sure you write a plan for your answers and back up your points with examples from the play. You know the drill.

## Exam-style Questions

1) How does Shakespeare create tension in the play?
   Refer to the extract below from Act 3, Scene 5 and to the play as a whole.

   | | |
   |---|---|
   | **Leonato:** | Neighbours, you are tedious. |
   | **Dogberry:** | It pleases your worship to say so, but we are the poor duke's officers. But truly, for mine own part, if I were as tedious as a king, I could find in my heart to bestow it all of your worship. |
   | **Leonato:** | All thy tediousness on me, ah? |
   | **Dogberry:** | Yea, an 'twere a thousand pound more than 'tis; for I hear as good exclamation on your worship as of any man in the city and though I be but a poor man, I am glad to hear it. |
   | **Verges:** | And so am I. |
   | **Leonato:** | I would fain know what you have to say. |
   | **Verges:** | Marry, sir, our Watch tonight, excepting your worship's presence, ha' ta'en a couple of as arrant knaves as any in Messina. |
   | **Dogberry:** | A good old man, sir. He will be talking — as they say 'when the age is in, the wit is out'. God help us, it is a world to see! Well said, i' faith, neighbour Verges. Well, God's a good man; an two men ride of a horse, one must ride behind. An honest soul, i' faith, sir; by my troth he is, as ever broke bread; but God is to be worshipped — all men are not alike, alas, good neighbour! |
   | **Leonato:** | Indeed, neighbour, he comes too short of you. |
   | **Dogberry:** | Gifts that God gives. |
   | **Leonato:** | I must leave you. |
   | **Dogberry:** | One word, sir: our Watch, sir, have indeed comprehended two aspicious persons, and we would have them this morning examined before your worship. |
   | **Leonato:** | Take their examination yourself and bring it me: I am now in great haste, as it may appear unto you. |

   (Act 3, Scene 5)

2) Read Act 3, Scene 1 from "**O, do not do your cousin such a wrong.**" to the end of the scene. How does Shakespeare present Beatrice in this extract and in the rest of the play?

3) Read Act 2, Scene 1 from "**Lady, will you walk about with your friend?**" to "**you are he, you are he.**" Then answer the questions below.

   **a)** How does Shakespeare create a lively atmosphere in this extract?

   **b)** In this extract, the audience sees a different side to Hero. Explore how Shakespeare presents the different sides to characters in other parts of the play. Write about:

   - the different sides to different characters seen in the play

   - how these different sides are shown to the audience.

# The Assessment Objectives

The assessment objectives are the basis for your exams — you need to meet them to get top marks.

## The exam questions will test four main skills

1) You will need to show the examiner that you can meet the following assessment objectives:

- **Assessment Objective One (AO1)** — show that you have **read** and **understood** the text, and give a **thoughtful**, **personal** response, **picking out** appropriate **examples** and **quotations** to back up your opinions.
- **Assessment Objective Two (AO2)** — **identify** and **explain** features of the text's **form**, **structure** and **language**. Show how the author uses these to create **meanings** and **effects**, using **subject terminology** where relevant.
- **Assessment Objective Three (AO3)** — relate the text to its **cultural**, **social and historical background**.
- **Assessment Objective Four (AO4)** — write in a **clear**, **well-structured**, **accurate** way. **5%** of the **total marks** in your English Literature exams are for **spelling**, **punctuation** and **grammar**.

*Different exam questions test different assessment objectives — see p.58.*

2) A good way to **improve exam technique** is to identify objectives you **struggle with** and try to improve them.

3) The table below shows how to meet the assessment objectives at **different grades**. Look at the **differences** between **each grade band**, and think about what you can do to **achieve the higher grades**.

| Grade band | Assessment Objective | An answer at this level... |
|---|---|---|
| 8-9 | AO1 | • shows an insightful, critical and engaged personal response to the text<br>• supports arguments with well-integrated, highly relevant and precise examples from the text |
| | AO2 | • closely and perceptively analyses in detail how the writer uses language, form and structure to create meaning and affect the audience, using highly relevant subject terminology |
| | AO3 | • gives a detailed, relevant explanation of the relationship between the text and its context |
| | AO4 | • uses highly varied vocabulary and sentence types and accurate spelling and punctuation |
| 6-7 | AO1 | • shows a critical and observant personal response to the text<br>• supports arguments with integrated, well-chosen examples from the text |
| | AO2 | • includes a thorough exploration of how the writer uses language, form and structure to create meaning and affect the audience, making use of appropriate subject terminology |
| | AO3 | • explores the relationship between the text and its context |
| | AO4 | • uses a wide range of vocabulary and sentence types and fairly accurate spelling and punctuation |
| 4-5 | AO1 | • shows a thoughtful and clear personal response to the text<br>• integrates appropriate examples from the text |
| | AO2 | • examines how the writer uses language, form and structure to create meaning and affect the audience, making some use of relevant subject terminology |
| | AO3 | • shows an understanding of contextual factors |
| | AO4 | • uses a moderate range of vocabulary and sentence types, without spelling and punctuation errors which make the meaning unclear |

## Assessment objectives — objectively useful...

Learning the text back-to-front will help you know *what* to write in your answers, but you also need to know *how* to answer the questions — that's where assessment objectives come in useful. Try to keep them in mind as you're revising.

# Preparing for the Exam

Getting to know the text will put you at a massive advantage in the exam. It's not enough to know the text really well though — you've also got to get familiar with the exam paper if you want to do well.

## Make sure you know what your exam looks like

1) There are some **differences** between how each **exam board examines** *Much Ado About Nothing*. For example, different exam boards test different assessment objectives in each question. You don't want to **waste time** trying to meet an assessment objective that **won't gain you marks**.

2) Check which exam board you're **entered** for and then have a look at the **table below**:

| | AQA | Edexcel | Eduqas | OCR |
|---|---|---|---|---|
| **Paper** | Paper 1 | Paper 1 | Paper 1 | Paper 2 |
| **Total time** | 1 hour 45 minutes | 1 hour 45 minutes | 2 hours | 2 hours |
| **Time for *Much Ado About Nothing*** | 55 minutes | 55 minutes | 1 hour | 45 minutes |
| **Question structure** | One question about an extract <u>and</u> the whole text | One two-part question. Part a) about an extract, part b) about the whole text | Two questions. One about an extract, one about the whole text | **EITHER** a question about an extract <u>and</u> the whole text **OR** a question on the whole text (no extract) |
| **Assessment objectives** | AO1, AO2, AO3, AO4 | AO1, AO2, AO3 | AO1, AO2, AO4 | AO1, AO2, AO3, AO4 |
| **Total marks** | 34 | 40 | 40 | 40 |

## Preparation is important

1) It's **important** to cover **all** the **different sections** of this book in your **revision**. You need to make sure you **understand** the text's **context**, **plot**, **characters**, **themes** and **writer's techniques**.

2) In the **exam**, you'll need to **bring together** your **ideas** about these topics to answer the question **quickly**.

3) Think about the different **characters** and **themes** in the text, and write down some **key points** and **ideas** about each one. Then, find some **evidence** to support each point — this could be something from **any** of the **sections** in this book. You could set out your evidence in a **table** like this:

| Theme: Deception and Misunderstanding | |
|---|---|
| **Drives the plot** | Don John's schemes cause conflict — he deceives Claudio, who then slanders Hero. Tricks bring the couples together. |
| **'Noting'** | Pun about noting in the title of the play highlights the trouble ("<u>Much Ado</u>") caused by noting and observing. |
| **Appearances are deceptive** | Characters are afraid that people aren't what they seem — "<u>seemed I ever otherwise to you?</u>" |

## Preparing to succeed — a cunning plot indeed...

Knowing the plot inside-out will be unbelievably helpful in the exam. It'll help you to stay calm and make sure you write a brilliant answer that positively glitters with little gems of evidence. The exam's just a chance for you to show off...

# The Exam Question

This page deals with how to approach an exam question. The stuff below will help you get started on a scorching exam answer, more scorching than, say, a phoenix cooking fiery fajitas in a flaming furnace.

## Read the question carefully and underline key words

1) The style of question you'll get depends on which **exam board** you're taking.

2) Read all the **instructions** carefully and make sure you know **how much time** you should spend on the Shakespeare question.

3) If the question has **more than one part**, look at the total number of marks for each bit. This should help you to plan your **time** in the exam.

4) **Read** the question at least **twice** so you completely understand it. **Underline** the key words. If you're given an **extract**, underline **important** words or phrases in that too.

*Henry didn't read the weather report carefully enough when planning his weekend activities.*

**Here's an example of an exam-style question:**

Remember to write about **form**, **structure** and **language**.

'**How** questions' ask you to think about the writer's **techniques**. E.g. Shakespeare's use of **characterisation** and **imagery**.

**Q1** How does Shakespeare present the theme of honour in the play?
Refer to the following extract in your answer...

Honour is a key **theme** — use a range of examples to support your answer.

You must **refer to** and **quote from** the extract in your answer.

> Different exam questions will ask you to write about either the extract, the text as a whole or both. Make sure you read the instructions carefully.

## Get to know exam language

Some **words** come up time and again in **exam questions**. Have a look at some **specimen** papers, pick out words that are **often used** in questions and make sure that you **understand** what they mean. You could **write a few down** whilst you're revising. For example:

| Question Word | You need to... |
|---|---|
| **Explore / Explain** | Show **how** the writer deals with a **theme**, **character** or **idea**. Make several **different** points to answer the question. |
| **How does** | Think about the **techniques** or **literary features** that the author uses to get their point across. |
| **Give examples** | Use direct quotes and describe events from the text in your own words. |
| **Refer to** | Read the question so that you know if you need to write about just an **extract**, or an extract and the **rest of the play**. |

## The advice squad — the best cops in the NYPD...

Whatever question you're asked in the exam, your answer should touch on the main characters, themes, structure and language of the text. All the stuff we've covered in the rest of the book in fact. It's so neat, it's almost like we planned it.

# Planning Your Answer

I'll say this once — and then I'll probably repeat it several times — it is absolutely, completely, totally and utterly essential that you make a plan before you start writing.  Only a fool jumps right in without a plan...

## Plan your answer before you start

*Read through the extract carefully and annotate it with some ideas to help you make your plan.*

1) If you plan, you're less likely to forget something **important**.

2) A good plan will help you **organise** your ideas — and write a good, **well-structured** essay.

3) Write your plan at the **top of your answer booklet** and draw a **neat line** through it when you've finished.

4) **Don't** spend **too long** on your plan.  It's only **rough work**, so you don't need to write in full sentences.  Here are a few **examples** of different ways you can plan your answer:

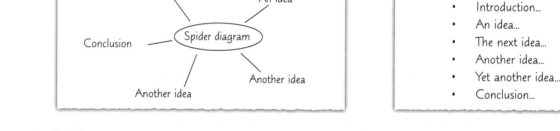

```
Introduction           An idea
Conclusion — (Spider diagram)
          Another idea    Another idea
```

```
Bullet points...
    •   Introduction...
    •   An idea...
    •   The next idea...
    •   Another idea...
    •   Yet another idea...
    •   Conclusion...
```

## Include bits of evidence in your plan

1) **Writing** your essay will be much **easier** if you include **important quotes** and **examples** in your plan.

2) You could include them in a **table** like this one:

3) **Don't** spend **too long** writing out quotes though.  It's just to make sure you **don't forget** anything when you write your answer.

| A point... | Quote to back this up... |
|---|---|
| Another point... | Quote... |
| A different point... | Example... |
| A brand new point... | Quote... |

## Structure your answer

```
Introduction
    ↓
Middle Section
— paragraphs
expanding
your
argument.
    ↓
Conclusion
```

1) Your **introduction** should give a brief answer to the question you're writing about.  Make it clear how you're going to **tackle the topic**.

2) The **middle section** of your essay should explain your answer in detail and give evidence to back it up.  Write a **paragraph** for each point you make.  Make sure you **comment** on your evidence and **explain how** it helps to **prove** your point.

3) Remember to write a **conclusion** — a paragraph at the end which **sums up** your **main points**.  There's **more** about introductions and conclusions on the **next page**.

*Dirk finally felt ready to tackle the topic.*

## To plan or not to plan, that is the question...

The answer is yes, yes, a thousand times yes.  Often students dive right in, worried that planning will take up valuable time.  But 5 minutes spent organising a well-structured answer is loads better than pages of waffle.  Mmm waffles.

# Writing Introductions and Conclusions

Now you've made that plan that I was banging on about on the last page, you'll know what your main points are. This is going to make writing your introduction and conclusion as easy as pie.

## Get to the point straight away in your introduction

1) First, you need to **work out** what the question is **asking you** to do:

> How is the character of Hero important to the play?

The question is **asking you** to think about the **role** of **Hero** in the play.
Plan your essay by thinking about **how** this character **links** to the play's **plot** and main **themes**.

2) When you've **planned** your essay, you should **begin** by giving a **clear answer** to the **question** in a sentence or two. Use the **rest** of the **introduction** to **develop** this idea. Try to include the **main paragraph ideas** that you have listed in your plan, but **save** the **evidence** for later.

3) You could also use the **introduction** to give your **opinion**. Whatever you do, make sure your introduction makes it **clear** how your answer **fits the question**.

## Your conclusion must answer the question

1) The **most important** thing you have to do at the **end** of your writing is to **summarise** your **answer** to the question.

2) It's your **last chance** to persuade the examiner, so make your **main point** again.

3) Use your **last sentence** to really **impress** the **examiner**. You could **develop** your own **opinion** of the text or **highlight** which of your **points** you thought was the most **interesting**.

The examiner was struggling to see the answer clearly.

## Use the exact question words in your introduction and conclusion

1) Try to use **words** or **phrases** from the **question** in your introduction and conclusion.

> How does Shakespeare present Margaret in the play?

2) This will show the examiner that you're **answering the question**.

> In 'Much Ado About Nothing', Shakespeare presents Margaret as a lower-status, witty serving woman. Although she has playful banter with Benedick, Hero and Beatrice, she is also unknowingly involved in Don John's plan.

The first line of the introduction gives a clear answer, which will lead on to the rest of the essay.

3) This will also help you keep the question **fresh in your mind** so your answer doesn't **wander off-topic**.

## I've come to the conclusion that I really like pie...

To conclude, the introduction eases the examiner in gently, whilst the conclusion is your last chance to impress. But remember — the examiner doesn't want to see any new points lurking in those closing sentences.

# Writing Main Paragraphs

So we've covered the beginning and the end, now it's time for the meaty bit. The roast beef in between the prawn cocktail and the treacle tart. This page is about how to structure your paragraphs. It's quite simple...

## P.E.E.D. is how to put your argument together

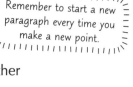

Remember to start a new paragraph every time you make a new point.

1) **P.E.E.D.** stands for: **P**oint, **E**xample, **E**xplain, **D**evelop.

2) Begin each paragraph by making a **point**. Then give an **example** from the text (either a quote or a description). Next, **explain** how your example backs up your point.

3) Finally, try to **develop** your point by writing about its effect on the audience, how it links to another part of the text or what the writer's intention is in including it.

## Use details from the text to back up your points

1) You can use **different** sorts of **examples** to support your points.

2) If you're using a **quote**, try to keep it **short**:

> It's best to use short, embedded quotes as evidence.

> Hero's criticisms during the trick make Beatrice question herself. She is surprised that Hero "condemned" her "so much" and decides to change.

> Don't just use quotes to describe the plot — it's much better to use them as evidence to support a point you're making.

3) **Quotes** are usually the **clearest** way to illustrate a point, but sometimes you can use a **paraphrased detail instead**. For example, you could briefly describe an **event** in the text:

> Shakespeare includes masks as symbols of deception throughout the play. For example, the characters conceal their identities at the masked ball, and this is paralleled when Hero wears a mask at her wedding in the final scene.

## Get to know some literary language

1) Using **literary terms** in your answer will make your essay stand out — as long as you use them correctly.

2) When you're **revising**, think about literary terms that are **relevant** to the text and how you might **include** them in an essay. Take a look at the table below for some examples.

> It's not enough to just name a feature — you should explain the effect that it has on the audience.

| Literary Term | Definition | Example |
|---|---|---|
| **Personification** | A figure of speech that talks about a thing as if it's a person. | "time goes on crutches" |
| **Simile** | Compares one thing to another, often using 'like' and 'as'. | "You seem to me as Dian in her orb" |
| **Metaphor** | Describing something by saying it is something else. | "his words are a very fantastical banquet" |

## This page is so exciting — I nearly...

Now now, let's all be grown-ups and avoid the obvious joke. It's a good way of remembering how to structure your paragraphs though. Point, Example, Explain, Develop. Simple. Maybe we could make a rap or something... anyone?

# Choosing Quotes

Whether you're looking at an extract or the whole text, quotes can go a long way to support your answer.

## Memorise useful quotes for the exam

1) It's really **important** to **learn quotes** that you can use in the exam.
   Make yourself a **bank** of quotes and examples that you can use to **support** your answers.

2) Here are some **tips** on how to **choose** the most **useful quotes** to memorise:

   - Choose quotes that are **relevant** to specific **characters** and **themes** — exam questions often focus on these topics.

   - Try to pick quotes with a **language** or **structural feature** that you can analyse.

   - Keep your quotes **as short as possible** — **cut out** anything **unnecessary**. This will make them **easier to remember** and you'll spend **less time** writing them out in the exam.

3) Here's an **example** of a **useful quote** that you could include in your quote bank:

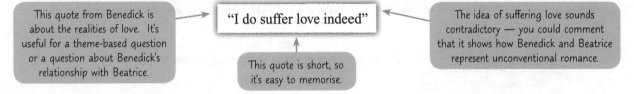

This quote from Benedick is about the realities of love. It's useful for a theme-based question or a question about Benedick's relationship with Beatrice.

"I do suffer love indeed"

This quote is short, so it's easy to memorise.

The idea of suffering love sounds contradictory — you could comment that it shows how Benedick and Beatrice represent unconventional romance.

## In extract questions, find quotes that match the question

1) If you're given an **extract** in the exam, read it **carefully** and **pick out** words or phrases that **link to the question**.

2) For example, if you were given a question on **Beatrice's attitude towards Benedick** and the extract below, there are lots of quotes you could use to show how her love is portrayed:

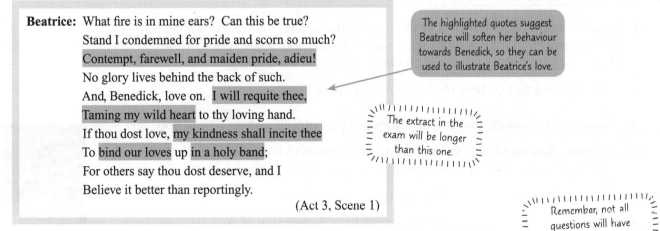

**Beatrice:** What fire is in mine ears? Can this be true?
Stand I condemned for pride and scorn so much?
Contempt, farewell, and maiden pride, adieu!
No glory lives behind the back of such.
And, Benedick, love on. I will requite thee,
Taming my wild heart to thy loving hand.
If thou dost love, my kindness shall incite thee
To bind our loves up in a holy band;
For others say thou dost deserve, and I
Believe it better than reportingly.

(Act 3, Scene 1)

The highlighted quotes suggest Beatrice will soften her behaviour towards Benedick, so they can be used to illustrate Beatrice's love.

The extract in the exam will be longer than this one.

3) Think about what these words and phrases **tell you** about the **topic** you're being asked to write about. Then use this to form the basis of your exam answer.

Remember, not all questions will have extracts — see page 58.

4) Focus on the bits of the extract that are **most relevant** to the question — you won't have time to cover the whole extract, so write about the **most important parts**.

5) If you're asked to refer to the **whole text**, remember to include **examples** that **aren't** from the extract too.

## This page is really useful — and you can quote me on that...

Quotes are completely essential to show the examiner that you know the text and can support your arguments. Don't try to write out half the play though — a short and snappy quote will often serve you better than a long one.

# In the Exam

Keeping cool in the exam can be tricky. But if you take in all the stuff on this page, you'll soon have it down to a fine art. Then you can stroll out of that exam hall with the swagger of an essay-writing master.

## Don't panic if you make a mistake

1) Okay, so say you've timed the exam beautifully. Instead of putting your feet up on the desk for the last 5 minutes, it's a good idea to **read through** your **answers** and **correct any mistakes**...

2) If you want to get rid of a mistake, **cross it out**. **Don't scribble** it out as this can look messy. Make any corrections **neatly** and **clearly** instead of writing on top of the words you've already written.

> techniques
> The author uses various literary ~~teknikues~~ to explore this theme.

This is the clearest way to correct a mistake. Don't be tempted to try writing on top of the original word.

3) If you've **left out** a **word** or a **phrase** and you've got space to add it in **above** the line it's missing from, write the missing bit above the line with a '^' to show exactly where it should go.

Re-read the sentence carefully to work out where the '^' symbol needs to go.

> and hyperbole
> The writer uses imagery^to draw attention to this point.

4) If you've left out whole **sentences** or **paragraphs**, write them in a **separate section** at the **end** of the essay. Put a **star** (*) next to both the **extra writing** and the **place** you want it to go.

## Always keep an eye on the time

1) It's surprisingly **easy** to **run out of time** in exams. You've got to leave **enough time** to answer **all** the questions you're asked to do. You've also got to leave enough time to **finish** each essay properly — with a **clear ending**.

2) Here are some **tips** on how to **avoid** running out of time:

- Work out **how much time** you have for each part of your answer **before** you **start**.
- Take off a few minutes at the beginning of the exam to **plan** your answer, and leave a **few minutes** at the end to write your **conclusion**.
- **Keep checking** the **clock** so you don't lose track of time.
- Be **strict** with yourself — if you spend **too long** on one part of your answer, you may run out of time. **Stick** to your **planned timings** as much as possible.
- If you're **running out of time**, keep **calm**, **finish** the **point** you're on and move on to your **conclusion**.

Stephanie never had a problem with keeping cool.

## Treat an exam like a spa day — just relax...

Some people actually do lose the plot when they get into the exam. The trick is to keep calm and well... carry on. If you make sure you get your exam technique sorted, you'll be as relaxed as a sloth in a room full of easy chairs.

# Sample Exam Question

And now the bit you've all been waiting for — a sample exam question and a lovely little plan.
Go and make yourself a cup of tea, then settle down and enjoy.

## Here's a sample exam question...

Read this feisty exam question. That's the best way to start...

*In the exam, you'll be given the full extract in the exam paper.*

**Read** the question carefully.
Underline the **important bits**.

**Back up** each point with **evidence** from the text and **analyse** why it's **important**.

Q1    In Act 2, Scene 1, read from the line beginning
"**Come, you shake the head**" to the end of the scene.

How does Shakespeare present Don Pedro in this extract and elsewhere in the play?

Think about the **language** that Don Pedro uses and his **behaviour** in the extract. Write about his **role** in the play and how the **audience** might react to his character.

You'll need to discuss the **extract** given **in detail** but you also need to refer to the **rest of the play**.

## Here's how you could plan your answer

*Make sure you don't spend too long planning — you need to leave plenty of time to write your answer.*

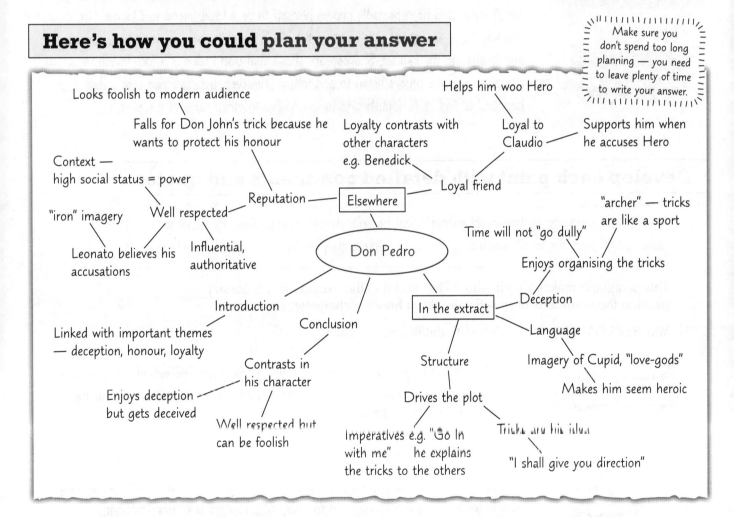

Looks foolish to modern audience

Falls for Don John's trick because he wants to protect his honour

Context — high social status = power

"iron" imagery

Leonato believes his accusations

Well respected

Influential, authoritative

Reputation

Loyalty contrasts with other characters e.g. Benedick

Helps him woo Hero

Loyal to Claudio

Supports him when he accuses Hero

**Elsewhere**

Loyal friend

**Don Pedro**

Introduction

Conclusion

Linked with important themes — deception, honour, loyalty

Enjoys deception but gets deceived

Contrasts in his character

Well respected but can be foolish

**In the extract**

Structure

Drives the plot

Imperatives e.g. "Go in with me"    he explains the tricks to the others

Time will not "go dully"

"archer" — tricks are like a sport

Enjoys organising the tricks

Deception

Language

Imagery of Cupid, "love-gods"

Makes him seem heroic

Tricks are his idea

"I shall give you direction"

## What do examiners eat? Why, egg-sam-wiches of course...

The most important thing to remember is DON'T PANIC. Take a deep breath, read the question, read it again, write a plan... take another deep breath... and start writing. Leave a few minutes at the end to check your answer too.

**Section Six — Exam Advice**

# Worked Answer

This bit will show you how to take an OK answer and turn it into a great one that will impress the examiner.

## Use your introduction to get off to a good start

*These pages are all about how to word your sentences to impress the examiner, so we haven't included everything from the plan on page 65.*

You might start with something like...

> Shakespeare presents Don Pedro as a high-status character who enjoys tricks and deception. He is responsible for bringing the couples together, and other characters follow his lead because he is influential and respected.

1) This intro is **okay**. It looks at the **character** of Don Pedro and how he is presented.

2) Using the **key words** from the question gives your essay **focus**, and shows the examiner you're on **track** and that you're thinking about the question from the start.

3) But there's still room for **improvement** — here's a better introduction...

*This tells the examiner that you've thought about Don Pedro's role in the play.*

> In 'Much Ado About Nothing', Shakespeare presents Don Pedro as the driving force behind the deceptions that bring the couples together. He enjoys playing tricks on his friends, but is nevertheless respected by the other characters because of his high social status and he repeatedly proves himself to be a loyal friend to Claudio. In this way, he is associated with some of the play's main themes — deception, honour and loyalty. In the extract, Shakespeare shows that Don Pedro is a fun-loving character who the others listen to and follow. However, the audience sees a less honourable and more foolish side to Don Pedro in other parts of the play.

*This shows a detailed understanding of Don Pedro's character.*

## Develop each point with detailed comments and quotes

> Don Pedro's language in the extract suggests that he finds deception enjoyable. He wants to gain "glory" from the tricks, which suggests that he thinks they will be exciting and entertaining.

1) This paragraph makes a **point** about Don Pedro in the extract. But it doesn't **develop** the point **fully** or give details about **how** his character is presented.

2) You should develop your points with **detail** and comments:

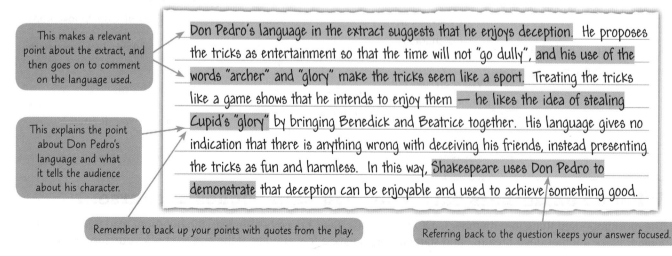

*This makes a relevant point about the extract, and then goes on to comment on the language used.*

*This explains the point about Don Pedro's language and what it tells the audience about his character.*

> Don Pedro's language in the extract suggests that he enjoys deception. He proposes the tricks as entertainment so that the time will not "go dully", and his use of the words "archer" and "glory" make the tricks seem like a sport. Treating the tricks like a game shows that he intends to enjoy them — he likes the idea of stealing Cupid's "glory" by bringing Benedick and Beatrice together. His language gives no indication that there is anything wrong with deceiving his friends, instead presenting the tricks as fun and harmless. In this way, Shakespeare uses Don Pedro to demonstrate that deception can be enjoyable and used to achieve something good.

*Remember to back up your points with quotes from the play.*

*Referring back to the question keeps your answer focused.*

# Worked Answer

## Write about the rest of the play

In this question, you can't just focus on the extract — you need to discuss Don Pedro **elsewhere** in the play.

> Shakespeare also presents Don Pedro as an influential character elsewhere in the play. When Hero is slandered, his support makes the accusations more believable because he is powerful and well respected.

1) This paragraph still focuses on how **Don Pedro** is **presented**, but discusses **the rest of the play**.

2) You can make this paragraph better by giving more **detailed examples** and backing up points with **quotes**.

> In other parts of the play, Don Pedro is also presented as influential. He is a prince, which means he has the highest social status of all the characters, and he is well respected, which leads the other characters to be influenced by him. In Act 4, Scene 1, when he joins Claudio in slandering Hero, his support makes the accusations more believable. Leonato rejects Hero — he asks "Would the two princes lie" and uses the imagery of something "barred up" with "iron" to show how strong he believes their accusations are. However, the audience knows that Don Pedro has been deceived and is making a mistake. Shakespeare shows that Don Pedro can still be foolish despite his influence, high status and honourable reputation.

*Don't forget to explain how your points link to the question.*

3) You could develop this by focusing on the **context** in which the play was written:

*Make sure your points about context are linked closely to the text and the question.*

> The Elizabethans believed in a strict social hierarchy. People were born with a certain status that was established by their lineage. A prince like Don Pedro had power and influence because he was near the top of the social hierarchy. As Don Pedro is easily deceived and wrongly slanders Hero, Shakespeare could be suggesting that status doesn't always equal wisdom.

*Not all exam boards give marks for context. See p.58 for more.*

## Finish your essay in style

You could say:
> In 'Much Ado About Nothing', Don Pedro is a well-respected character who enjoys trickery and deception. However, he also makes mistakes and is deceived by Don John.

1) This conclusion is okay but it doesn't summarise **how** Shakespeare presents Don Pedro.

2) So to make it really **impressive** you could say something like...

> In the extract, Shakespeare presents Don Pedro as a well-respected prince who enjoys deception. This might seem like a contradiction, but Don Pedro's dramatic description of the tricks suggests that deception can be harmless. However, elsewhere in the play, Don Pedro behaves foolishly and demonstrates the dangers of deception — he falls for his brother's lies and slanders Hero. The audience sees the irony in the contrasting ways that Don Pedro is presented. He is influential and respected but sometimes foolish — a man who deceives others but isn't immune to being deceived.

*This shows that you've considered different aspects of Don Pedro's character*

*Make your final sentence really stand out — it's your last opportunity to impress the examiner.*

## Why do alligators write good essays? Their quotes are so snappy...

It seems like there's a lot to remember on these two pages, but there's not really. To summarise — write a scorching intro and a sizzling conclusion, make a good range of points (one per paragraph) and include plenty of examples. Easy.

# Exam Tips

We've scoured examiners' reports and mark schemes, and come up with these tips for doing well. Here's a breakdown of what the markers like to see (cake) and what they don't like to see (Brussels sprouts).

## Here are our top 10 things to do in the exam...

1) **Do** make sure you **know the text** really well before you go into the exam.

2) **Do** come up with your own **interpretations** of the text that can be **supported** with evidence.

3) **Do read and reread** any extract really carefully, and check that you're **referring** to it correctly in your answer.

4) **Do plan** your answer. It helps you **organise** your thoughts and give a clear response.

5) **Do** write about **how** an **extract relates** to the text as a whole (**if** you're asked to discuss **both**) — think about **where** in the text it comes, and what happens before and after.

6) **Do** remember to comment on **structure** and **form** as well as language.

7) **Do eat** a really good **breakfast** before the exam. Maybe some **porridge** — try adding some strawberries, blueberries, Dogberries... Yum.

8) **Do** write about **why** the author **chose** to use the **words** they do — think about the **effects** they may have been trying to create.

9) **Do** remember to write about **context** in your answer **if** it's being tested in the question. Make sure the context is **relevant** and **clearly linked** to the text.

10) **Do** use **short quotes** from the text to **save time** and make your answer **clear**.

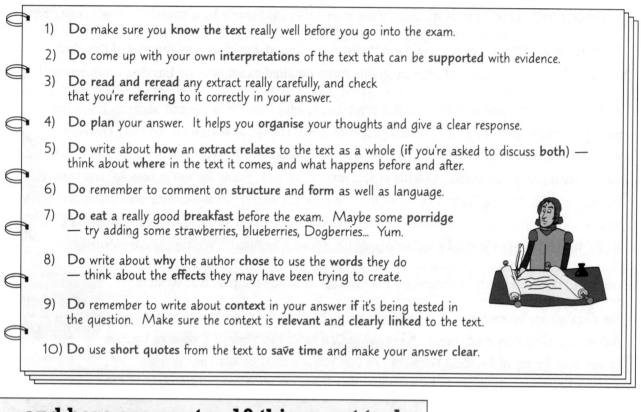

## ... and here are our top 10 things not to do

1) **Don't** just **rewrite** an **essay** that you've **written before** the exam — it might not be answering the **question** properly and the points you make might not be **relevant**.

2) **Don't** answer the question that you **wish** had been asked — make sure you **answer the question** that **has** been asked.

3) **Don't** just **name the techniques** being used — you need to **explain the effect** they have too.

4) **Don't** jump straight into answering the question **without planning**.

5) **Don't contradict yourself** or change your mind halfway through — this can make your points seem weak. It's fine to **discuss two sides** of an argument, but you need to come to a **clear conclusion** at the end.

6) **Don't** write your whole answer about a specific passage in the text — **unless** the question asks you to.

7) **Don't** write about quotes in a way that **misinterprets** what they mean in the text, and don't **shoehorn** them in when they don't fit your argument. This will make it seem like you don't know the text.

8) **Don't** dress like you're going to a masked ball — there's a time and a place for that (Renaissance Italy).

9) **Don't cram** loads of **points** into each paragraph — stick to a structure like P.E.E.D. instead (see p.62).

10) **Don't** include **unnecessary context** if it doesn't link to the question or your argument.

# Complete the Plan

t's time to put your exam knowledge into practice. You'll find answers for this whole section in your Online Edition — to access it, just go to **cgpbooks.co.uk/extras** and enter the code at the front of this book.

## Complete the Plan

The question type and answers shown here are similar to the AQA and OCR exams. If you're doing another exam board, you can find a version that suits you by redeeming your online edition.

- Below is an **exam question** and a blank **plan**. Draw your **own version** on a separate **piece of paper**.
- Think of **four points** that could go in the 'Point' column to answer the exam question.
- Find **examples** from the text to back up each of your points for the 'Evidence' column. Make sure you use a **mixture** of examples from the extract and the rest of the text.
- You **don't** need to write the answer itself — just come up with a plan.

1) Read the following extract from *Much Ado About Nothing* and answer the question that follows. At this point in the play, the characters are waiting for the guests to arrive at the masked ball.

**Antonio:** (*To Hero*) Well, niece, I trust you will be ruled by your father.

**Beatrice:** Yes, faith. It is my cousin's duty to make curtsy and say 'Father, as it please you.' But yet for all that, cousin, let him be a handsome fellow, or else make another curtsy and say 'Father, as it please me.'

**Leonato:** Well, niece, I hope to see you one day fitted with a husband.

**Beatrice:** Not till God make men of some other metal than earth. Would it not grieve a woman to be overmastered with a piece of valiant dust? To make an account of her life to a clod of wayward marl? No, uncle, I'll none. Adam's sons are my brethren, and, truly, I hold it a sin to match in my kindred.

**Leonato:** Daughter, remember what I told you — if the Prince do solicit you in that kind, you know your answer.

**Beatrice:** The fault will be in the music, cousin, if you be not wooed in good time. If the Prince be too important, tell him there is measure in every thing and so dance out the answer. For, hear me, Hero — wooing, wedding, and repenting, is as a Scotch jig, a measure, and a cinque pace: the first suit is hot and hasty, like a Scotch jig, and full as fantastical; the wedding, mannerly-modest, as a measure, full of state and ancientry; and then comes repentance and, with his bad legs, falls into the cinque pace faster and faster, till he sink into his grave.

(Act 2, Scene 1)

How does Shakespeare present Beatrice as strong-willed in *Much Ado About Nothing?*

Write about:

- how Shakespeare presents Beatrice as strong-willed in this extract
- how Shakespeare presents Beatrice as strong-willed in the rest of the play.

Remember — you would need to explain and develop your points if you wrote out your answer in full.

| Point | Evidence |
|---|---|
| | |
| | |
| | |
| | |

# Improve the Answer

Now it's time to have a go at choosing examples. Look back at page 63 for advice on selecting quotes.

## Add Examples

You can refer to your copy of the play to help you with this question.

- Below are some parts of **sample answers** for another exam-style question.
- Find a **quote** or **example** from the text that could fill each gap below (marked **A-H**).

> 1) Read Act 4, Scene 1, from "**I talked with no man at that hour**" to "**HERO** *swoons*".
> At this point in the play, Claudio has accused Hero of infidelity.
> Using this extract as a starting point, explore how Shakespeare presents ideas about appearance and reality.
>
> Write about:
> - how Shakespeare presents ideas about appearance and reality in this extract
> - how Shakespeare presents ideas about appearance and reality in the play as a whole.

1) When Claudio denounces Hero in this extract, he comments on the apparent contradiction between her innocent appearance and supposedly corrupt reality. He uses two oxymorons: **(A)** and **(B)**. These contradictory phrases emphasise the large gap between Claudio's initial perception of Hero and what he believes to be reality. This helps the audience to understand some of the reasons why he is so shocked and angry at her supposed betrayal.

2) In the extract, the gap between appearances and reality is used to create dramatic irony. Don Pedro's speech to Leonato contains dramatic irony; the audience knows that his belief that he saw her **(C)** doesn't reflect reality. Through this dramatic irony, Shakespeare creates tension for the audience, as they know that reality is not as it appears to be and the characters have been deceived. The tension is then increased as Leonato believes Don Pedro, asking **(D)**. His extreme response shows that the consequences of Don John's trick are likely to be extremely serious.

3) At the start of the play, Benedick gives the appearance of being dismissive of women, but Shakespeare implies that this isn't the entire truth. In Act I, Scene I, when Claudio asks for Benedick's opinion of Hero, Benedick asks if Claudio wants his **(E)** or if he should speak as a **(F)** towards women. This distinction suggests that the way Benedick talks about women isn't reflective of his real feelings. This foreshadows his character development over the course of the play: by the end, Benedick has dropped his false appearance as someone who dislikes women and openly professes love for Beatrice instead.

4) Beatrice is a character who disguises the reality of her feelings. Despite her teasing of Benedick early in the play, Shakespeare suggests that she for cares for him. For example, although she mocks him in her first line, calling him **(G)**, the fact that she immediately checks whether he is safe from the war suggests that she cares about his welfare. She later hints that she and Benedick previously had a relationship, but says he won her heart with **(H)**. The gambling metaphor suggests that Benedick 'cheated' Beatrice in some way, which hints that she hides the reality of her feelings because he hurt her before.

# Improve the Answer

's time for even more activities on improving answers — this time on developing points and adding context.

## Develop the Points

> To develop your point you could write about its effect on the audience, how it links to another part of the text or what the writer's intention is in including it.

- Below are some more parts of **sample answers** for the question on page 70.
- Write an extra sentence that could go in each gap (marked **A-C**) to develop the points.

1) Don John's behaviour in the extract shows how the appearance of politeness can be used to conceal reality. He begs Don Pedro not to describe Hero's actions because "There is not chastity enough in language" to say them "Without offence". This polite language makes it seem as though Don John is shocked by Hero's supposed actions when in reality he knows they never happened. **(A)**

2) The play shows that misleading appearances can have a significant effect on characters' lives. For example, during, Act 2, Scene 1, the characters attend the masked ball. The masks allow the characters to take on false appearances, such as when Don Pedro is able to pretend to be Claudio and woo Hero. This is an important moment in the play, as it leads to Claudio's marriage, which is a key part of the plot. **(B)**

3) The tricks played on Beatrice and Benedick show that the act of disguising reality can sometimes be an enjoyable one. During these tricks, Claudio says of Benedick: "this fish will bite", and Ursula calls Beatrice a "fish" who will "greedily devour the treacherous bait". These metaphors create a humorous tone that suggests the other characters find fun in blurring the lines between appearance and reality. **(C)**

## Add Context

> You might not need to include context (AO3) in your exam on 'Much Ado About Nothing' — check the table on p.58.

- Below are some more parts of **sample answers** for the question on page 70.
- Write an extra sentence for each gap (marked **A-B**) that links the answer to the context of the play.

1) During the wedding scene, Claudio uses classical references to highlight the difference between Hero's appearance and what he believes to be her true self. He says that Hero appears to be like "Dian in her orb" but is actually "more intemperate" than "Venus". In Roman mythology, these two goddesses represent two opposites: **(A)**. By using these classical references, Claudio is trying to elevate his language and make his accusations seem more serious. But the effect on the audience is ironic: it is clear that Hero is as "chaste" as she appears, and it is actually Claudio's accusations that obscure the truth.

2) Hero's public appearance contrasts with how she is in private. During the opening scenes, Hero has few lines and acts submissively, but in the company of her waiting ladies she speaks openly. At the start of Act 3, Hero plans the trick on Beatrice with a speech in blank verse. She uses a simile to describe the honeysuckles as "like favourites, / Made proud by princes". This elaborate, poetic language shows her eloquence and intelligence, which shows that much of her personality is hidden when she is in the company of men. **(B)**

# Mark the Answer

Here's another sample question, and this time there's a full answer to sink your teeth into (delicious).

## Mark the Answer

Once you're done, turn to p.86 in the online edition to find out what grade this answer would get and why.

- Below is an exam question and a sample answer.

- The sample answer has been annotated, showing where it has done well or not so well for each assessment objective. Add some more annotations to show what's good and what could be improved.

- Decide whether you think the answer belongs in the grade band **4-5**, **6-7** or **8-9** (see page 57).

- Give at least **three reasons** why you've decided on that grade band.

---

1) Read Act 1, Scene 1, from "**Benedick, didst thou note...**" to "**... if Hero would be my wife.**" At this point in the play, Don Pedro and his men have just arrived at Leonato's house.

   Starting with this extract, write about how Shakespeare presents the theme of love and marriage in *Much Ado About Nothing*.

   Write about:

   - how ideas about love and marriage are presented in this extract
   - how ideas about love and marriage are presented elsewhere in the play.

---

In this extract and the rest of the play, Shakespeare presents different approaches to love and marriage by contrasting the conventional route taken by Claudio and Hero and the unorthodox path taken by Benedick and Beatrice. These relationships, as well as the conventions of the comedy genre, ultimately criticise courtly love and present love and marriage as undermining male friendships.

> **AO4**: This uses a good variety of vocabulary and sophisticated sentence types.

In the extract, Claudio follows the conventions of courtly love, a way of showing love that was common among the higher classes in Shakespeare's time. A courtly lover was expected to be infatuated with the woman he loved, and to write poems or songs to praise her. Like a traditional courtly lover, Claudio is infatuated with Hero, describing her poetically as a "jewel". This metaphor shows that he sees her as something unique and highly valued. However, he joins Benedick in discussing whether he would "buy" (marry) Hero. This use of monetary language hints that, despite Claudio's idealistic love for Hero, he also recognises the financial and political benefits that marriage to her would bring.

Benedick, on the other hand, represents a more critical view of love and marriage. In the extract, he undermines Claudio's metaphor: when Claudio asks "Can the world buy such a jewel?", he responds "Yea, and a case to put it into." This mundane response shows that Benedick is less inclined to idealise women and has a more cynical view of love. Later in this scene, he says a married man must "wear his cap with suspicion". This is a reference to cuckolds: Elizabethans joked that men who had unfaithful wives grew horns and wore a cap to hide them. Benedick's words suggest that he believes all wives are unfaithful, which shows his cynicism about marriage.

> **AO3**: This shows a good understanding of the context the play was written in, and links this to the argument.

The answer continues on the next page...

# Mark the Answer

However, Benedick's dismissive attitude towards love changes when he overhears that Beatrice loves him. For example, in Act 4, Scene 1, he calls her "Lady Beatrice", where previously he had mocked her with epithets such as "Lady Disdain". By addressing her politely using her title and name, Benedick shows respect for Beatrice, which reflects how his attitude towards her is changing. However, even after this change, he still represents an unconventional attitude towards love. In Act 5, Scene 2, he attempts to follow the conventions of courtly love and write a poem for Beatrice, but fails, saying he "cannot woo in festival terms." The adjective "festival" links the act of courtly love to parties and merriment, which could make the audience view courtly love as more frivolous than Benedick's love for Beatrice. Benedick's example therefore reveals a measured attitude to love: a middle ground between the courtly lover and the dismissive bachelor.

> AO2: This examines the language of the extract in detail.

The conventions of the comedy genre are used to comment on love and marriage in the play. Claudio is initially presented as the romantic hero; he claims to "love" Hero moments after their first encounter in the play, which is a common feature of a Shakespearean comedy. As a result, the audience expects the play to be solely about Claudio's love story with, and eventual marriage to, Hero. However, Claudio and Hero share no lines together on stage before their wedding day, whereas Benedick and Beatrice "are too wise to woo peaceably" and engage in witty banter. As a result, an audience might see Claudio and Hero's love as more shallow and less compelling than the relationship between Beatrice and Benedick. This surprises the audience by moving the plot in a different direction to their initial expectations, and therefore encourages them to question their existing ideas about what ideal love and marriage look like.

Throughout the play, love and marriage are presented as being in conflict with male social bonds. For example, in Act 2, Scene 3, Benedick laments that Claudio's love for the "drum" and "fife" (powerful music associated with the military) has been replaced by the "tabor" and "pipe" (gentle music associated with romance). An Elizabethan audience would have recognised the contrast between these two types of music, so this highlights Claudio's move towards romantic love and marriage, and the weakening of his masculine bond with Benedick. The conflict between love and male friendship comes to a climax when Beatrice commands Benedick to "Kill Claudio" to prove his love for her. The use of an imperative highlights the shocking nature of this demand. When Benedick agrees to challenge Claudio, it is the most significant act of love in the play: he is willing to go against his own beliefs about the importance of male social bonds and kill his close friend in order to win Beatrice's love.

> AO1: The analysis is engaged and insightful, and concludes with a more personal response.

In the extract from the beginning of the play, Claudio is set up to be the conventional romantic hero. However, Benedick's growth and his relationship with Beatrice provide a contrast to Claudio's shallow relationship with Hero, challenge preconceptions about love and marriage, and highlight the conflict between love and male bonds. While the play does end with a celebration of love and marriage, the audience is left with the clear impression that unorthodox love is more desirable than conventional courtly love.

# Index

# The Characters in 'Much Ado About Nothing'

Phew!  You should be an expert on *Much Ado About Nothing* by now.  But if you want a bit of light relief and a quick recap of what happens in the play, read through *Much Ado About Nothing — The Cartoon...*

Benedick

Beatrice

Hero

Claudio

Don Pedro

Leonato

Don John

Friar Francis

Dogberry

Borachio

Conrade

# William Shakespeare's 'Much Ado About Nothing'